MW01030274

# BASICS OF KEYBOARD THEORY

# LEVEL 7

Fifth Edition

Julie McIntosh Johnson

J. Johnson Music Publications

5062 Siesta Lane
Yorba Linda, CA 92886
Phone: (714) 961-0257
Fax: (714) 242-9350
www.bktmusic.com
info@bktmusic.com

**Basics of Keyboard Theory, Level 7, Fifth Edition**

Published by:

J. Johnson Music Publications
5062 Siesta Ln.
Yorba Linda, CA 92886 U.S.A.
(714) 961-0257
www.bktmusic.com

©2014 by Julie McIntosh Johnson. Revised.
Previous editions ©1983, 1992, 1997. and 2007, Julie McIntosh Johnson.
Printed in United States of America

**Library of Congress Cataloging in Publication Data**

Johnson, Julie Anne McIntosh
Basics of Keyboard Theory, Level 7, Fifth Edition

ISBN 10: 1-891757-07-5
ISBN 13: 978-1-891757-07-5

LC TX 4-721-497

*Basics of Keyboard Theory, Level 7 corresponds with the MTAC Certificate of Merit™ Piano Syllabus. Certificate of Merit™ is an evaluation program of the Music Teachers' Association of California. Reference to 'Certificate of Merit™' (CM) does not imply endorsement by MTAC of this product.*

# TO THE TEACHER

Intended as a supplement to private or group music lessons, *Basics of Keyboard Theory, Level 7* presents basic theory concepts to the early advanced music student. This level is to be used with the student who has had approximately seven to eight years of music lessons, and is playing piano literature at the level of Mozart's *Sonata, K. 545*, or Beethoven's *Sonata, Op. 49, No. 2*.

*Basics of Keyboard Theory, Level 7* is divided into sixteen lessons, with two reviews, and a test at the end. Application of each theory concept is made to piano music of the student's level. Lessons may be combined with one another or divided into smaller sections, depending on the ability of the student. Whenever possible, it is helpful to demonstrate theory concepts on the keyboard, and apply them to the music the student is playing.

Learning music theory can be a very rewarding experience for the student when carefully applied to lessons. *Basics of Keyboard Theory, Level 7* is an important part of learning this valuable subject.

Also available from
J. Johnson Music Publications

# Julie Johnson's Guide to
# AP<sup>*</sup> Music Theory

by
Julie McIntosh Johnson
Author of *Basics of Keyboard Theory*

- Follows requirements of the College Board Advanced Placement* Music Theory exam
- Clear, easy to understand explanation of theory elements
- Application of concepts to musical excerpts
- Drills, analysis and multiple choice questions
- Ear training and sight singing with each lesson
- CD and answers included
- Purchase at your music store or order online

*AP and Advanced Placement are trademarks registered and/or owned by the College Board, which was not involved in the production of, and does not endorse, this product.

# TABLE OF CONTENTS

*Basics of Keyboard Theory* is dedicated to my husband Rob,
without whose love, support, help, and incredible patience,
this series would not have been possible.

# LESSON 1
# MAJOR AND MINOR KEY SIGNATURES

The **KEY SIGNATURE** for a musical composition is found at the beginning, next to the clef signs.

The **KEY SIGNATURE** indicates two things:

  1. The **key** or **tonality** of the music.

  2. Which notes in the music are to receive sharps or flats.

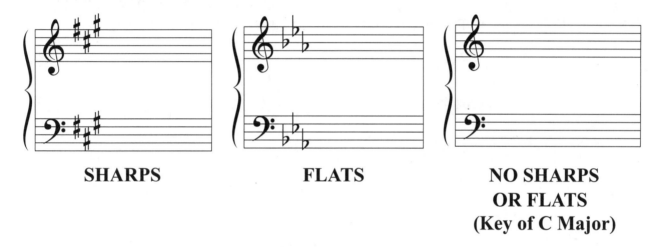

**SHARPS**      **FLATS**      **NO SHARPS OR FLATS (Key of C Major)**

If the key signature has <u>SHARPS</u>, they will be written in this order, on these lines and spaces. This is called the **ORDER OF SHARPS**.

FCGDAEB

**THE ORDER OF SHARPS**

A saying to help you remember this order is:

**Fat Cats Go Down Alleys Eating Bologna**

If a key signature has one sharp, it will be F♯. If a key signature has two sharps, they will be F♯ and C♯, etc.

To determine which Major key a group of sharps represents, find and name the last sharp (the sharp furthest to the right), then go up a half step from that sharp. The note which is a half step above the last sharp is the name of the Major key.

Three sharps:  F♯, C♯, G♯

Last sharp is G♯

A half step above G♯ is A

Key of A Major

To determine which sharps are in a Major key, find the sharp which is a half step below the name of the key. Name all the sharps from the Order of Sharps up to and including that sharp.

Key of D Major

A half step below D is C♯

Name all sharps, from the Order of Sharps, up to and including C♯

F♯ and C♯

If a key signature has <u>FLATS</u>, they will be in the following order, written on these lines and spaces. This is called the **ORDER OF FLATS.**

BEADGCF

**THE ORDER OF FLATS**

The Order of Flats can be memorized this way:

**BEAD Gum Candy Fruit**

If a key signature has one flat, it will be B♭. If it has two flats, they will be B♭ and E♭, etc.

To determine which Major key a group of flats represents, name the next to last flat.

Three flats:  B♭, E♭, A♭

Next to last flat is E♭

Key of E♭ Major

To determine which flats are needed for a given key, name all the flats from the Order of Flats up to and including the name of the key, then add one more.

Key of E♭ Major

Name all flats from the Order of Flats up to and including E♭, then add one more.

B♭, E♭, A♭

The key signature for F Major has to be memorized. It has one flat: B♭.

**KEY SIGNATURE FOR F MAJOR**

Major keys which have sharps will be named with a letter only, or a letter and a sharp (for example, G Major, D Major, F♯ Major).

Major keys which have flats will have a flat in the name (for example, B♭ Major, D♭ Major, E♭ Major).

The two exceptions to the above rules are F Major (one flat: B♭), and C Major (no sharps or flats).

4

1. Name these Major keys.

_____     _____     _____     _____     _____

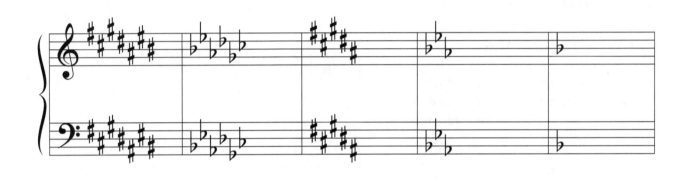

_____     _____     _____     _____     _____

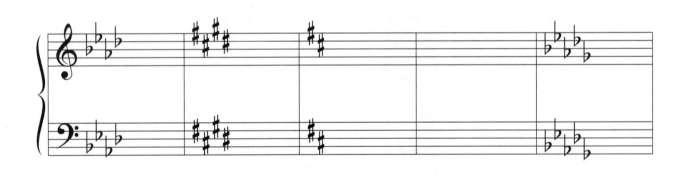

_____     _____     _____     _____     _____

2. Write the key signatures for these Major keys.

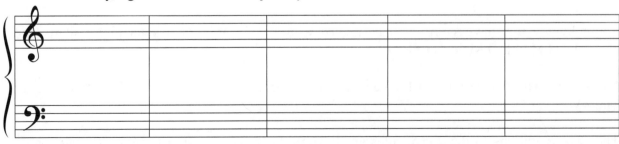

G Major          F♯ Major          F Major          D Major          B Major

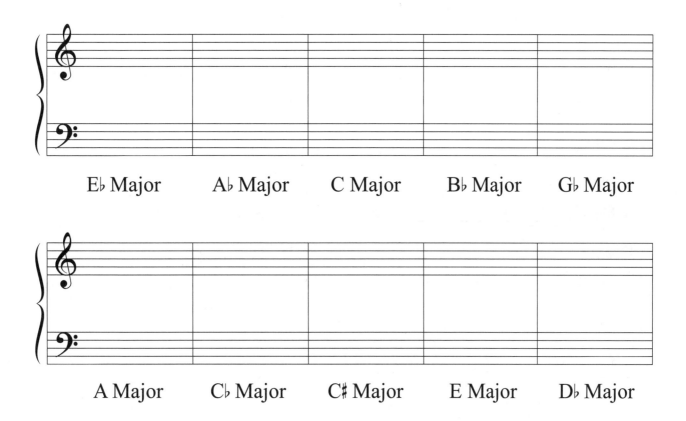

| Eb Major | Ab Major | C Major | Bb Major | Gb Major |

| A Major | Cb Major | C# Major | E Major | Db Major |

Most Major key signatures have **<u>RELATIVE MINORS</u>**. The relative minor is found by going down three half steps from the name of the Major key. Skip one letter between the names of the keys.

### KEY SIGNATURE FOR D MAJOR
### THREE HALF STEPS BELOW D IS B
### KEY OF B MINOR

One way to determine whether a composition is in the Major or minor key is to look at the last note. It is usually the same as the name of the key. (For example, music that is in the key of e minor will probably end on E.) Also, look for the note around which the music appears to be centered; which note appears to be the main note of the composition. This should be the same as the name of the key.

6

3. Write the name of the relative minor for each of the following Major keys.

G Major _____          A Major _____

E♭ Major _____         E Major _____

C Major _____          D♭ Major _____

F Major _____          B Major _____

B♭ Major _____         C♭ Major _____

D Major _____          G♭ Major _____

A♭ Major _____

4. Write the name of the relative Major for each of the following minor keys.

d minor _____          b minor _____

e minor _____          c♯ minor _____

f minor _____          b♭ minor _____

c minor _____          g♯ minor _____

a minor _____          e♭ minor _____

f♯ minor _____          a♭ minor _____

g minor _____

5. Name these minor keys. (Determine the name of the Major key, then go down three half steps to find the relative minor.)

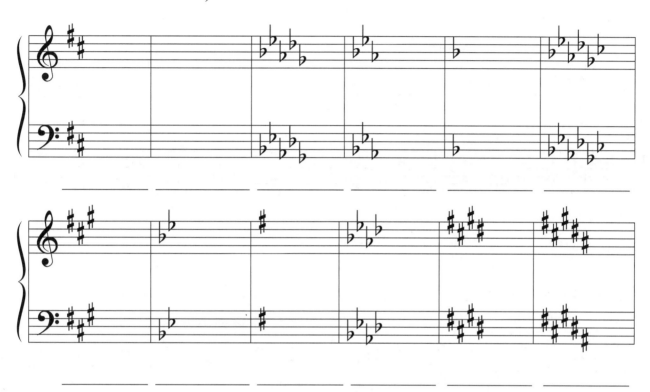

_____   _____   _____   _____   _____   _____

6. Write the key signatures for these minor keys. (Go up three half steps to find the relative Major, then write the key signature for that Major key.)

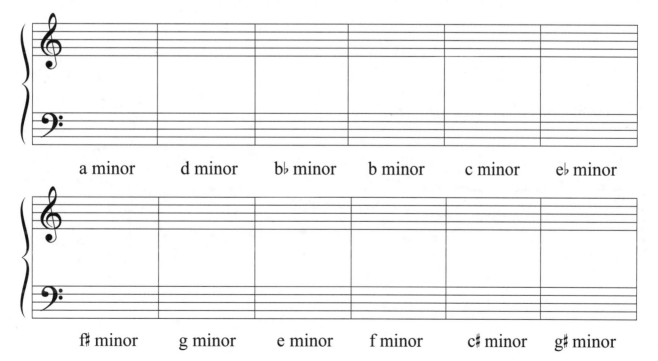

a minor     d minor     b♭ minor     b minor     c minor     e♭ minor

f♯ minor     g minor     e minor     f minor     c♯ minor     g♯ minor

8

7. Name the Major or minor key for each of the following examples.

a. From *Roundelay* by Schumann. _____ _____

b. From *Arietta* by Grieg. _____ _____

c. From *Mazurka, Op. 67, No. 2*, by Chopin. _____ _____

d. From *Mazurka, Op. 7, No. 1,* by Chopin. _____  _____

e. From *Prelude, Op. 28, No. 6,* by Chopin. _____  _____

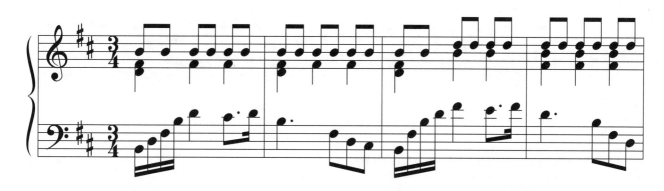

f. From *Prelude, Op. 28, No. 20,* by Chopin. _____  _____

g. From *Mazurka, Op. 39, No. 10,* by Tchaikovsky. _____ _____

h. From *Little Prelude No. 5* by J.S. Bach. _____ _____

8. Memorize these key signatures.

| C Major and a minor | No sharps or flats |
|---|---|
| G Major and e minor | F♯ |
| D Major and b minor | F♯ C♯ |
| A Major and f♯ minor | F♯ C♯ G♯ |
| E Major and c♯ minor | F♯ C♯ G♯ D♯ |
| B Major and g♯ minor | F♯ C♯ G♯ D♯ A♯ |
| F♯ Major and d♯ minor | F♯ C♯ G♯ D♯ A♯ E♯ |
| C♯ Major | F♯ C♯ G♯ D♯ A♯ E♯ B♯ |
| F Major and d minor | B♭ |
| B♭ Major and g minor | B♭ E♭ |
| E♭ Major and c minor | B♭ E♭ A♭ |
| A♭ Major and f minor | B♭ E♭ A♭ D♭ |
| D♭ Major and b♭ minor | B♭ E♭ A♭ D♭ G♭ |
| G♭ Major and e♭ minor | B♭ E♭ A♭ D♭ G♭ C♭ |
| C♭ Major and a♭ minor | B♭ E♭ A♭ D♭ G♭ C♭ F♭ |

The **CIRCLE OF FIFTHS**\* (sometimes called the **Circle of Keys**) is a method of organizing the Major and minor keys so that when ascending by perfect fifths from key to key, one sharp is added to each new key. When the keys of B, F♯, and C♯ are reached, there is an <u>enharmonic</u> change (notes with the same pitch but different letter names, such as F♯ and G♭). Flats are then used, and as the keys ascend by perfect fifths, one flat is deleted from each key.

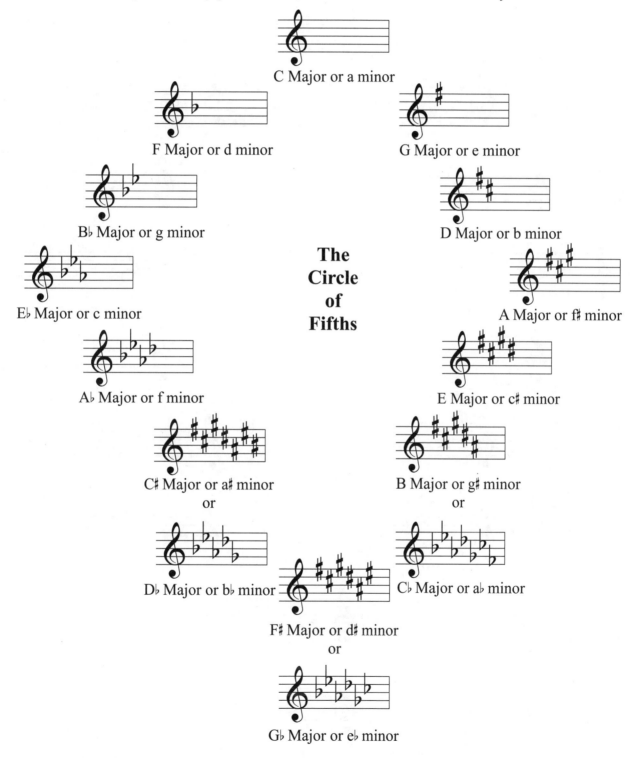

\*The Circle of Fifths may also be referred to as the Circle of Fourths. Moving counterclockwise through the chart demonstrates the Circle of Fourths.

12

9. Fill in the Circle of Fifths (Circle of Keys) below. Include the Major and minor key names, enharmonic equivalents, and write each key signature on the staff.

# LESSON 2
# SCALES

<u>SCALES</u> are made up of a series of notes, which are each a step apart. They begin and end with notes of the same letter name.

<u>MAJOR SCALES</u> contain eight notes, and have all the sharps or flats from the Major key signature with the same name.

Example: D Major Scale begins and ends with the note "D," and has F♯ and C♯. (In Major scales, most of the steps are whole steps, with half steps occuring between notes 3-4 and 7-8.)

## D MAJOR SCALE

There are three different forms of minor scales: <u>Natural Minor</u>, <u>Harmonic Minor</u>, and <u>Melodic Minor</u>.

<u>NATURAL MINOR SCALES</u> contain all the sharps or flats from the minor key signature with the same name.

Example: d natural minor scale begins and ends with the note "D," and has B♭.

## D NATURAL MINOR SCALE

<u>HARMONIC MINOR SCALES</u> are created by raising the seventh note of the natural minor scale a half step. This creates a half step, rather than a whole step, between the seventh and eighth notes of the scale, making the seventh a "leading tone."

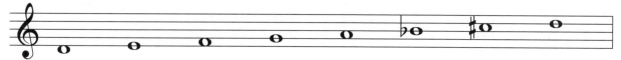

## D HARMONIC MINOR SCALE

<u>MELODIC MINOR SCALES</u> are created by raising the sixth and seventh notes of the natural minor scale while ascending, and returning them to natural minor (lowering them) while descending.

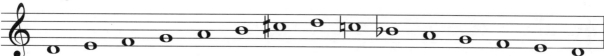

## D MELODIC MINOR SCALE

14

The **CHROMATIC SCALE** is a series of thirteen notes. Each note is a half step away from its neighbor. Using sharps while the scale is ascending and flats while the scale is descending prevents the use of many naturals, and makes the scale easier to read.

## CHROMATIC SCALE BEGINNING ON F

The **WHOLE TONE SCALE** consists entirely of whole steps. There are only seven notes in the whole tone scale, so when writing the scale on the staff, one letter name will be missing.

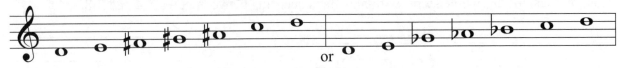

or

## WHOLE TONE SCALE ON D

**IONIAN MODE** is the same as the Major scale. Half steps occur between notes 3-4 and 7-8.

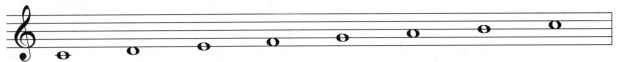

### IONIAN MODE ON C - SAME AS MAJOR SCALE

**DORIAN MODE** contains the pattern of whole and half steps that occur when beginning and ending on the second note of the Major scale. Half steps occur between notes 2-3 and 6-7.

### DORIAN MODE - BEGINS ON 2nd NOTE OF MAJOR SCALE

**MIXOLYDIAN MODE** contains the pattern of whole and half steps that occur when beginning and ending on the fifth note of the Major scale.. Half steps occur between notes 3-4 and 6-7.

### MIXOLYDIAN MODE ON G - BEGINS ON 5th NOTE OF MAJOR SCALE

**AEOLIAN MODE** has the same pattern of whole and half steps as the natural minor scale, or when beginning and ending on the second note of the Major scale. Half steps occur between notes 2-3 and 5-6.

### AEOLIAN MODE ON A - SAME AS NATURAL MINOR

**Instructions for finding modes on any note are on page 135.**

1. Write these scales.

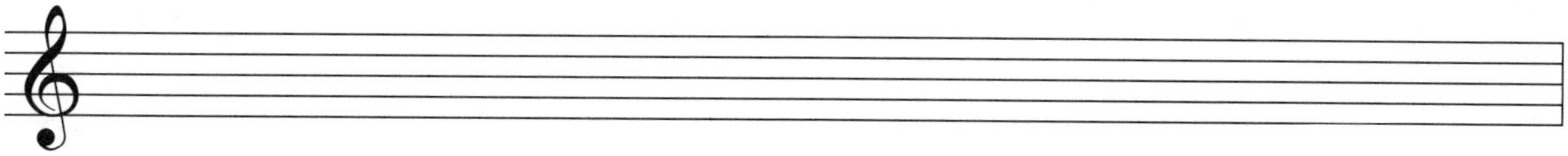

Cb Major

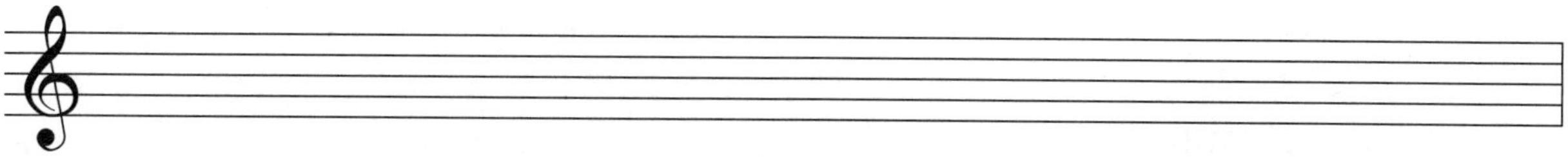

f# melodic minor (ascending and descending)

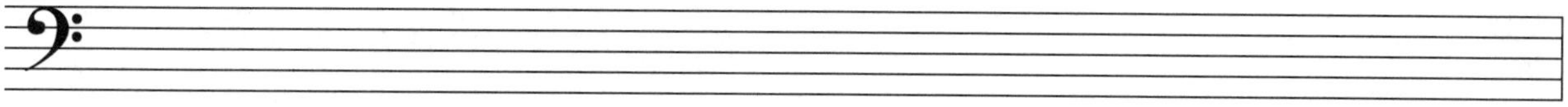

B Major

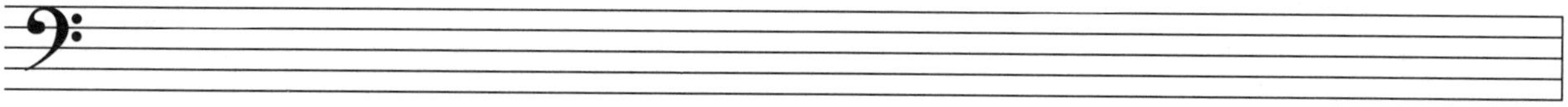

c# harmonic minor

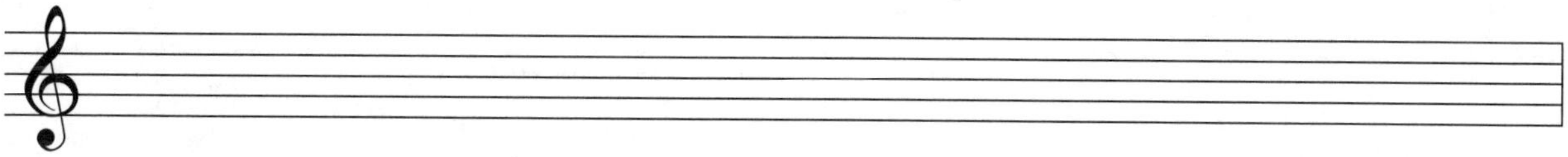

Eb Major

bb natural minor

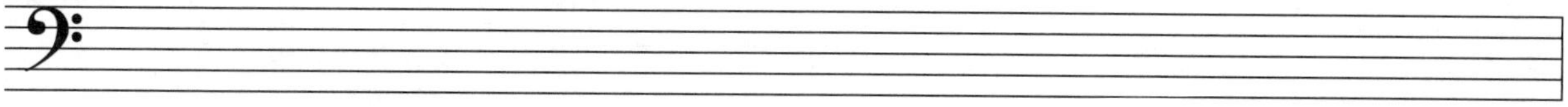

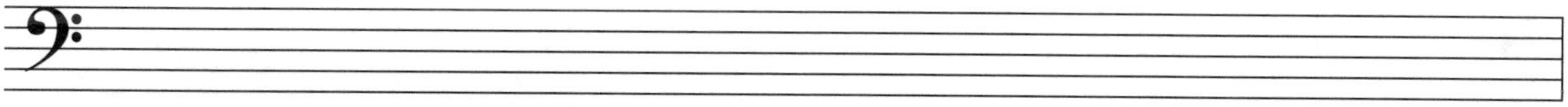

Whole tone beginning on B

A♭ Major

b natural minor

F♯ Major

g harmonic minor

C♯ Major

Chromatic scale beginning on G♯ (ascending and descending)

Aeolian mode beginning on A

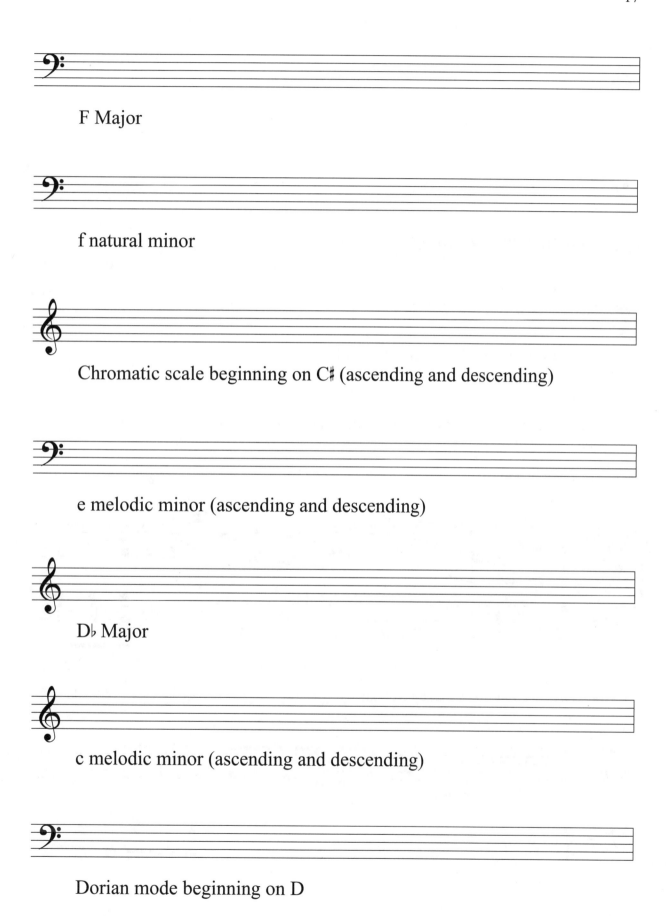

F Major

f natural minor

Chromatic scale beginning on C♯ (ascending and descending)

e melodic minor (ascending and descending)

D♭ Major

c melodic minor (ascending and descending)

Dorian mode beginning on D

18

Chromatic scale beginning on E (ascending and descending)

Ionian mode beginning on C

Mixolydian mode beginning on G

2. Name each of the circled scales with its name and type. For minor scales, include the form of minor.

a. From *Sonatina, Op. 20, No. 1*, by Kuhlau. _____ Scale

b. From *Sonatina, Op. 20, No. 2*, by Kuhlau. _____ Scale

19

c. From *Sonatina, Op. 20, No. 3*, by Kuhlau. _____ Scale

d. From *Sonatina, Op. 55, No. 2*, by Kuhlau. _____ Scale

e. From *The Water Wheel, Op. 41, No. 2,* by Lynes. _____ Scale

f. From *Album for the Young, Op. 68, No. 30* (Untitled), by Schumann.

_____ Scale

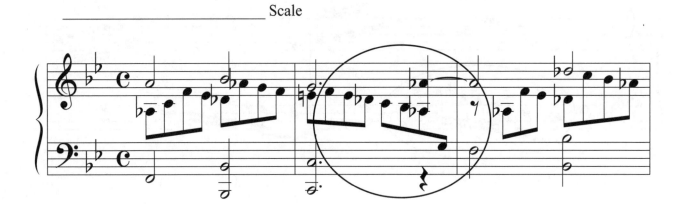

g. From *Mazurka, Op. 67, No. 2*, by Chopin. _____ Scale

h. From *Short Prelude*, BWV 926, by J.S. Bach. _____ Scale

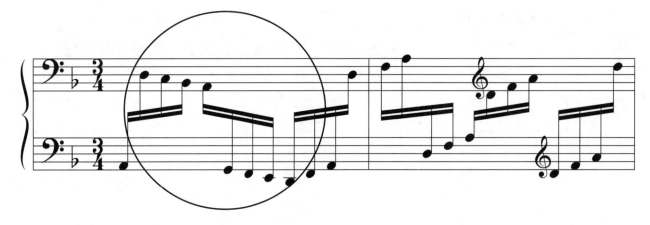

# LESSON 3
# INTERVALS

An **INTERVAL** is the distance between two notes.

Intervals are named with qualities and numbers.

When naming intervals, count the two notes that make the interval, and all the lines and spaces, or all the letter names, between the two.

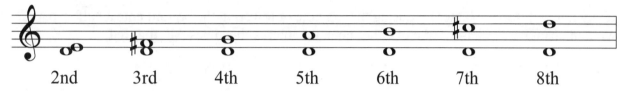

If the top note of the interval is within the key of the bottom note, the interval is **Major** or **Perfect**. 2nds, 3rds, 6ths, and 7ths are Major. 4ths, 5ths, and 8ths are Perfect.

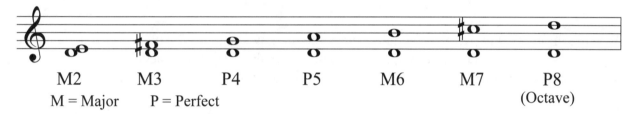

If a Major 2nd, 3rd, 6th, or 7th is made smaller by lowering the top note or raising the bottom note a half step, without changing the letter name of either note, the interval becomes **minor.**

If a Perfect 4th, 5th, or 8th (octave) is made smaller by lowering the top note or raising the bottom note a half step, without changing the letter name of either note, the interval becomes **diminished.**

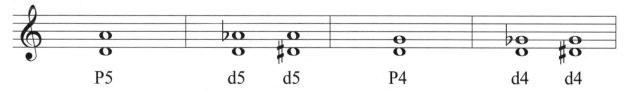

22

If a Major 2nd, 3rd, 6th, or 7th is made smaller by lowering the top note or raising the bottom note a whole step, without changing the letter name of either note, the interval becomes **diminished.**

If any interval is made larger by raising the top note or lowering the bottom note a half step, without changing the letter name of either note, the interval becomes **Augmented.**

To write an interval above a given note, determine the key signature for the lower note, and add any necessary accidentals. For Major or Perfect intervals, keep those accidentals. For minor, diminished, or Augmented intervals, raise or lower the top note without changing the letter name.

In the example below, an Augmented 4th above F is needed. F Major has B♭. The 4th is made Augmented by removing the B♭ (raising the note a half step).

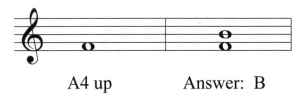

To write an interval below a given note, determine all possibilities the note could be. Then, determine which of those notes is the correct one for the quality of the interval needed.

In the example below, a minor 7th below C is needed. The three possibilities are D, D♭, and D♯. A minor 7th above D♭ is C♭, a minor 7th above D♯ is C♯, and a minor 7th above D is C. The answer is D.

1. Name each of these intervals with its quality and number. The first one is given.

   m3 _____ _____ _____ _____ _____ _____ _____

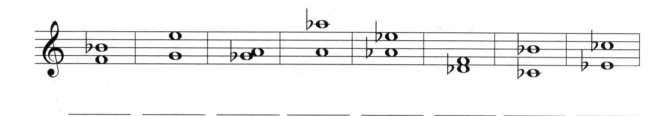

_____ _____ _____ _____ _____ _____ _____ _____

2. Complete each of these intervals. Do not change the given note.

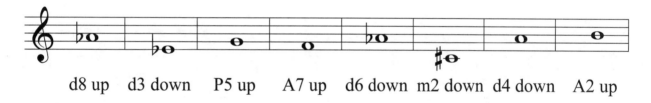

d8 up   d3 down   P5 up   A7 up   d6 down   m2 down   d4 down   A2 up

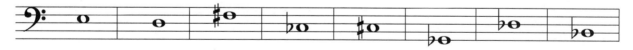

A3 down   A5 up   m6 down   M2 up   P4 down   M7 up   P8 down   A8 up

24

When naming intervals within music literature, follow these steps:

a. Write the sharps or flats from the key signature or from earlier in the measure before the notes. (This way, you will not forget to consider them while naming the interval.)

b. Determine the number for the interval (by counting the lines and spaces, or the letter names).

c. Using the key signature for the lowest note of the interval, find the quality (Major, minor, Perfect, diminished, or Augmented).

3. Name the circled intervals in the passages below. Follow the steps listed above for each one.

a. From *Arietta* by Grieg.

b. From *Prelude, Op. 28, No. 6,* by Chopin.

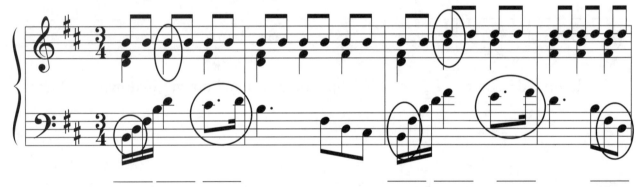

c. From *Little Prelude No. 5* by J.S. Bach.

# LESSON 4
# MAJOR, MINOR AUGMENTED AND DIMINISHED TRIADS AND INVERSIONS

A **TRIAD** is a three note chord, based on the interval of a third.

**D Major Triad**

**MAJOR TRIADS** are made up of the first, third, and fifth notes of the Major scale with the same name. The lowest note of a Major triad in root position names the triad.

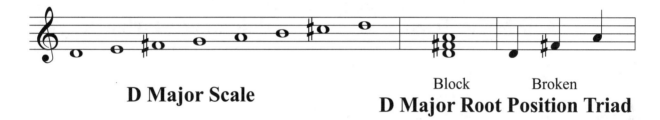

**D Major Scale**

Block     Broken
**D Major Root Position Triad**

To change a Major triad into a **MINOR** triad, lower the middle note (the third) a half step. Minor triads have the same sharps or flats as the minor key signature with the same name.

**D Major Triad**        **d minor triad**

To change a Major triad into an **AUGMENTED** triad, raise the top note (the fifth) a half step. The intervals between the notes are both Major 3rds.

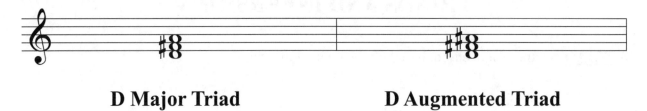

**D Major Triad**                    **D Augmented Triad**

To change a Major triad into a **DIMINISHED** triad, lower the middle note (the third) <u>and</u> the top note (the fifth) a half step each. The intervals between the notes are both minor 3rds.

**D Major Triad**                    **d diminished triad**

1. Write these triads.

gb dim.      c dim.      Eb Maj.      ab dim.      E Aug.      G Aug.

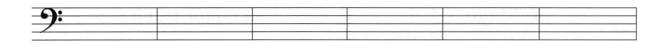

C# Maj.      f# min.      B Aug.      d min.      A Maj.      f min.

2. Name each of the following triads with its root and quality. The first one is given.

g dim.  _____  _____  _____  _____  _____

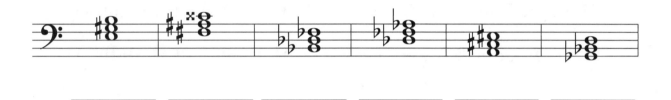

_____  _____  _____  _____  _____  _____

A **ROOT POSITION TRIAD** occurs when the note which names the triad is lowest.
**FIGURED BASS** is used to indicate the position or inversion. The figured bass for root position is $\frac{5}{3}$, because when the triad is in its simplest position, the intervals from the lowest note are a 5th and a 3rd. When labeling a triad in root position, only the letter name and quality are needed. The use of $\frac{5}{3}$ is optional.

**D Major Root Position Triad**

**D Major or D Major $\frac{5}{3}$**

A **FIRST INVERSION TRIAD** occurs when the **third** or **middle** note of the triad is lowest. The figured bass for first inversion is $^6_3$, because when the triad is in its simplest position (with the notes close together) it contains the intervals of a 6th and a 3rd above the lowest note.

When labeling first inversion triads, the symbol 6 or $^6_3$ is written to the right of the name of the triad.

**D Major Root Position Triad**

D Major or D Major $^5_3$

**D Major First Inversion Triad**

D Major $^6$ or D Major $^6_3$

A **SECOND INVERSION TRIAD** occurs when the **fifth** or **top** note of the triad is lowest. Second inversion triads are called $^6_4$ triads, because when they are in their simplest position (with the notes close together) they contain the intervals of a 6th and a 4th above the lowest note.

When labeling second inversion triads, the symbol $^6_4$ is written to the right of the name of the triad.

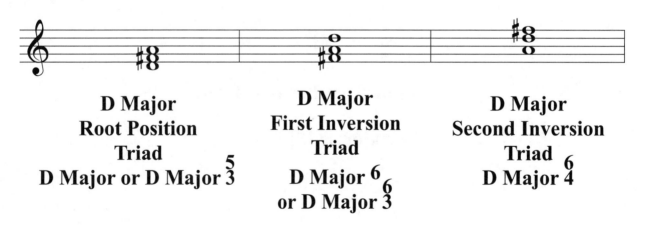

**D Major**
**Root Position**
**Triad**
D Major or D Major $^5_3$

**D Major**
**First Inversion**
**Triad**
D Major $^6_6$
or D Major $^6_3$

**D Major**
**Second Inversion**
**Triad**
D Major $^6_4$

3. Write these triads in root position, first inversion, and second inversion. The first one given.

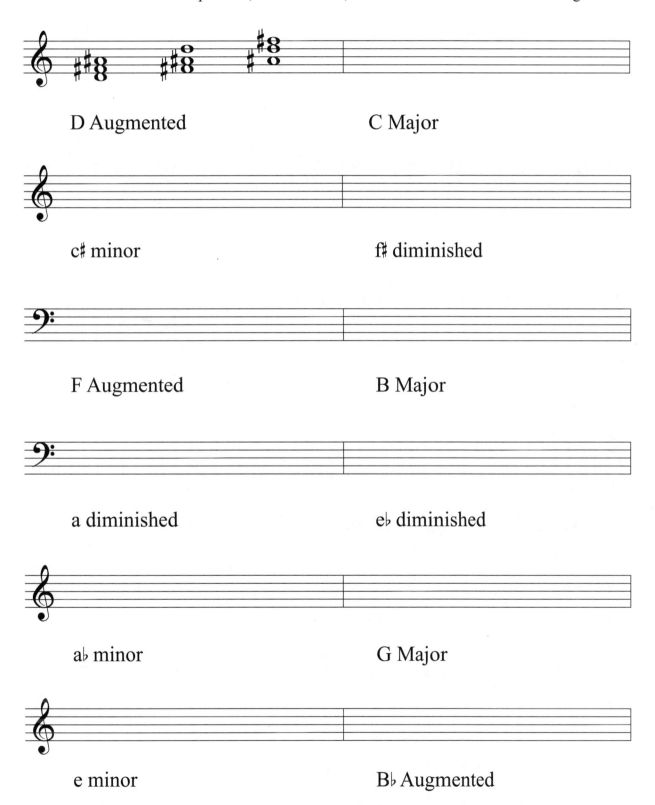

D Augmented                    C Major

c♯ minor                       f♯ diminished

F Augmented                    B Major

a diminished                   e♭ diminished

a♭ minor                       G Major

e minor                        B♭ Augmented

30

4. Name these triads with their roots, qualities, and figured bass. The first one is given.

Gb Major $\frac{6}{4}$ _____ _____ _____ _____ _____

_____ _____ _____ _____ _____ _____

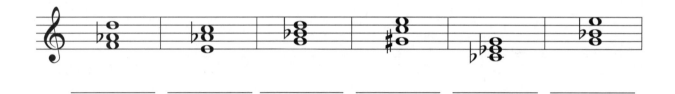

_____ _____ _____ _____ _____ _____

5. Write these triads.

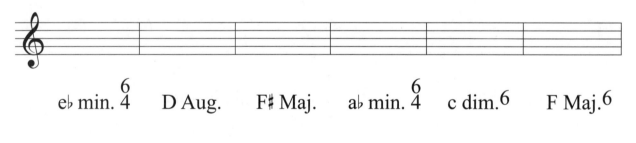

eb min. $\frac{6}{4}$     D Aug.     F# Maj.     ab min. $\frac{6}{4}$     c dim.$^6$     F Maj.$^6$

c# dim.$^6$     a min.$^6$     b min. $\frac{6}{4}$     Db Aug.     G Maj. $\frac{6}{4}$     d min.

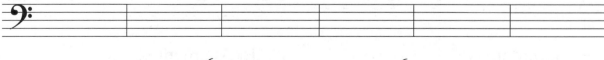

gb min.$^6$     bb min. $\frac{6}{4}$     f min.     Cb Maj. $\frac{6}{4}$     E Maj.     G Aug.$^6$

In actual music, triads are rarely in their simplest positions. To determine the root and quality of a triad within a composition, follow these steps:

a. Put the triad in its simplest form by placing the letter names so that there is one letter between each (for example, F-C-F-A becomes F-A-C).

b. Add all sharps or flats from the key signature, or from earlier in the measure, to the letter names.

c. Determine the root and quality of the triad.

d. Determine the inversion of the triad by looking at the lowest note on the <u>lowest</u> staff.

Example (From *Minuet in G* by Beethoven):

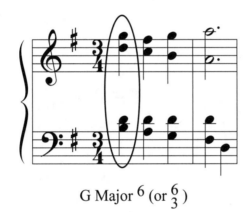

a. Notes are B-D-D-G.

b. Simplest form is G-B-D.

c. G Major Triad.

d. B is the lowest note (in the bass clef), so the triad is in first inversion ( $^6_3$ ).

e. G Major $^6$ (or G Major $^6_3$)

G Major $^6$ (or $^6_3$ )

If only two notes are present in a chord, and when they are simplified they create the interval of a third, they will most likely be the root and third of the chord, not the third and fifth. If one note occurs twice, it is most likely the root. (See examples 1 and 3.)

If the two notes create the interval of a fifth when simplified, they will be the root and fifth. (See example 2.)

Ex. 1. G Major Triad
Root and Third

Ex. 2. G Major Triad
Root and Fifth

Ex. 3. G Major Triad
Third and Fifth

Common

Occasional

Rare

32

6. Name each circled triads in the examples with root, quality, and figured bass.

a. From *Roundelay* by Schumann

———  ———  ———  ———  ———  ———

b. From *Mazurka, Op. 67, No. 2,* by Chopin.

———  ———  ———  ———

c. From *Prelude, Op. 28, No. 20,* by Chopin.

———  ———  ———  ———  ———  ———

———

# LESSON 5
# PRIMARY AND SECONDARY TRIADS

A triad can be built on each note of the scale.

When building triads on scale tones, all of the sharps or flats from the key with the same name are added to the chords which have those notes.

Example: D Major Scale has F♯ and C♯. When writing the triads of D Major, every time an F or C appears in a chord, a sharp is added.

Triads of the scale are numbered using Roman numerals. Upper case Roman numerals are used for Major triads, lower case Roman numerals are used for minor triads, upper case Roman numerals with "+" are used for Augmented triads, and lower case Roman numerals with "○" are used for diminished triads.

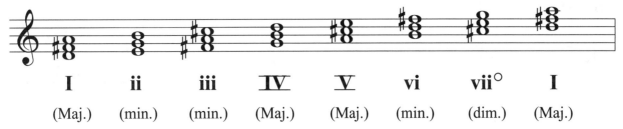

|  I  |  ii  |  iii  |  IV  |  V  |  vi  |  vii°  |  I  |
|:---:|:----:|:-----:|:----:|:---:|:----:|:------:|:---:|
| (Maj.) | (min.) | (min.) | (Maj.) | (Maj.) | (min.) | (dim.) | (Maj.) |

**PRIMARY AND SECONDARY TRIADS IN THE KEY OF D MAJOR**

**I, IV, and V** are the **PRIMARY TRIADS**. In Major keys, these three triads are Major, and are the most commonly used chords for harmonizing tonal melodies. The chords are labeled with upper case Roman numerals.

**ii, iii, vi, and vii°** are the **SECONDARY TRIADS**. In Major keys, ii, iii, and vi are minor, and vii° is diminished. The chords are labeled with lower case Roman numerals, and the vii° chord has a small circle beside the Roman numeral.

The qualities of the triads in minor keys are different from those for Major keys. When using **harmonic minor**, the triads have the following qualities:

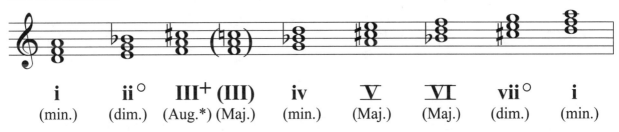

|  i  |  ii°  |  III⁺ (III)  |  iv  |  V  |  VI  |  vii°  |  i  |
|:---:|:-----:|:------------:|:----:|:---:|:---:|:------:|:---:|
| (min.) | (dim.) | (Aug.*) (Maj.) | (min.) | (Maj.) | (Maj.) | (dim.) | (min.) |

**PRIMARY AND SECONDARY TRIADS IN THE KEY OF D MINOR**

*Typically, the Augmented III (III⁺) chord is not used in minor keys. The III chord is usually Major.

34

1. Write the primary and secondary triads for these keys, and label the triads with Roman numerals. Circle each primary triad, and put a box around each secondary triad. Do not use a key signature. Write the sharps or flats before the notes. (The first one is given.)

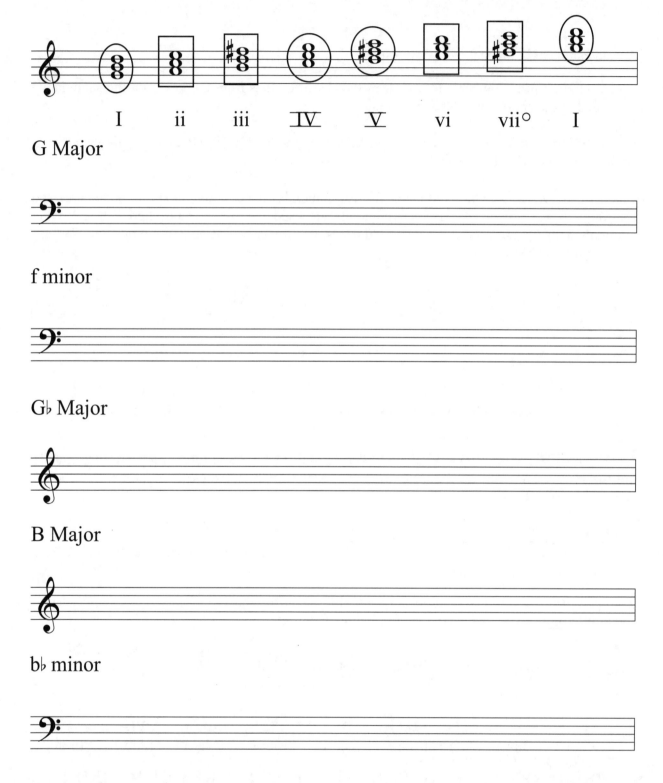

I    ii    iii    IV    V    vi    vii°    I

G Major

f minor

G♭ Major

B Major

b♭ minor

c♯ minor

2. Write the primary triads for these keys, and label them with Roman numerals. Do not use a key signature. Write the sharps or flats before the notes. (The first one is given.)

g minor     i      iv      V

E Major

F♯ Major              f♯ minor

e minor              D♭ Major

E♭ Major            b minor

36

3. Write the secondary triads for these keys, and label them with Roman numerals. Do not use a key signature. Write the sharps or flats before the notes. (The first one is given.)

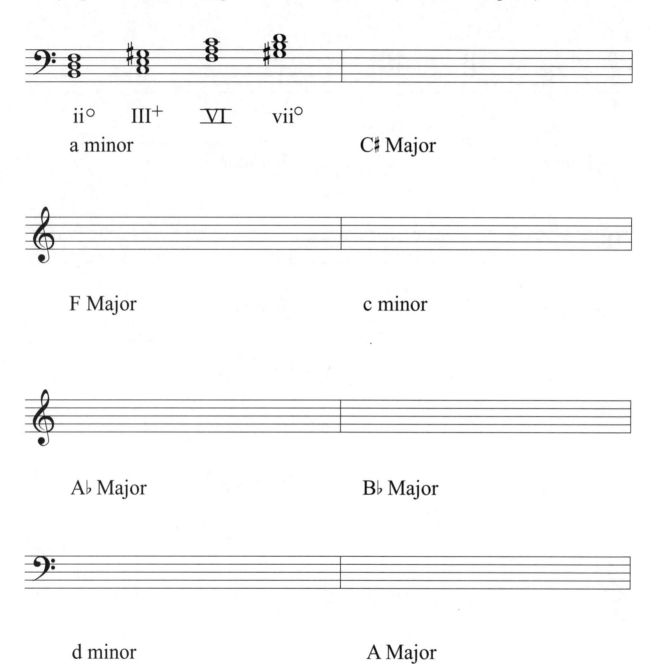

    ii°      III⁺    VI    vii°

a minor                           C♯ Major

F Major                           c minor

A♭ Major                        B♭ Major

d minor                           A Major

Each degree of the scale has a name. These are called the **SCALE DEGREE NAMES:**

The **I** chord is **TONIC**.

The **ii** chord is **SUPERTONIC**.

The **iii** chord is **MEDIANT**.

The **IV** chord is **SUBDOMINANT**.

The **V** chord is **DOMINANT**.

The **vi** chord is **SUBMEDIANT**.

The **vii°** chord is **LEADING TONE**.

(Note: Qualities used above are from Major keys. The names stay the same when in minor.)

4. Match these Roman numerals with their scale degree names.

a. ii _____ Submediant

b. I _____ Dominant

c. iii _____ Supertonic

d. vii° _____ Subdominant

e. IV _____ Leading Tone

f. vi _____ Mediant

g. V _____ Tonic

5. Write the scale degree names for these Roman numerals.

I _____

ii _____

iii _____

IV _____

V _____

vi _____

vii° _____

In actual music, chords are rarely in their simplest position. To determine the Roman numeral of a chord within a composition, follow these steps:

a.  Determine the Major or minor key.

b.  Put the chord in its simplest form by placing the letter names so that there is one letter between each (for example, F-C-F-A becomes F-A-C).

c.  Add all sharps or flats from the key signature or from earlier in the measure to the letter names.

d.  Determine the Roman numeral of the chord by counting from the letter name of the key up to the name of the chord.

e.  Determine the inversion of the chord by looking at the lowest note (on the <u>lowest</u> staff).

Example (From *Minuet in G* by Beethoven):

$$\underline{V}\,^6$$
$$\text{or } \underline{V}\,^6_3$$

a.  Key of G Major

b.  Notes are:  F♯-D-A-A

c.  Simplest form is:  D-F♯-A

d.  D Major Triad. The music is in the key of G Major. D is the fifth note of the G Major Scale; therefore, this is the $\underline{V}$ chord.

e.  The lowest note (in the bass clef) is F♯. The chord is in first inversion. Label the chord $\underline{V}\,^6$ or $\underline{V}\,^6_3$.

6. Name the Major or minor key for each of the following examples. Label each boxed chord
   with its Roman numeral and figured bass.

a. From *Sonatina, Op. 20, No. 1,* by Kuhlau..   Key of: _____

_____        _____              _____     _____

b. From *French Suite No. 5:  Gavotte*, by J.S. Bach. Key of: _____

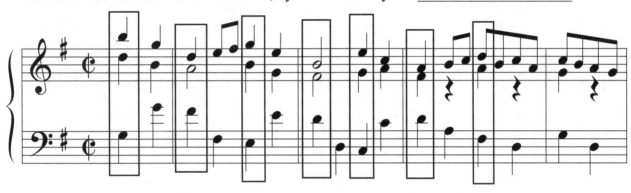

_____   _____   _____                _____        _____

c. From *Sonatina, Hob. XVI:4,* by Haydn. Key of: _____

_____        _____              _____           _____

40

d. Key of: _____

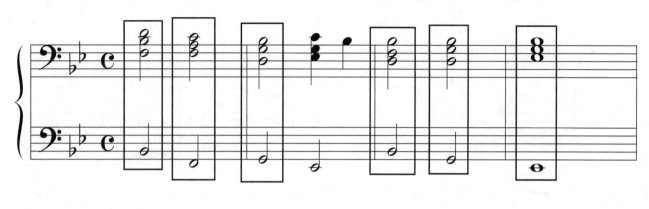

____ ____ ____    ____ ____ ____

e. From *Sonata, Op. 49, No. 2,* by Beethoven. Key of: _____

____    ____ ____ ____    ____

f. From *May, Sweet May,* by Schumann. Key of: _____

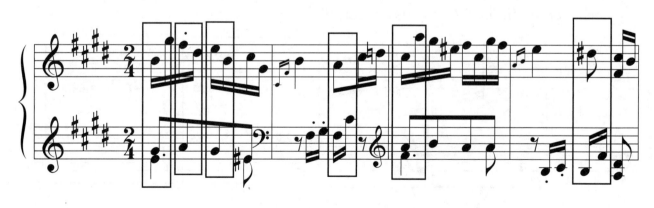

____ ____ ____    ____ ____

# LESSON 6
# DOMINANT AND DIMINISHED SEVENTH CHORDS

The **<u>DOMINANT SEVENTH CHORD</u>** is created by adding a note to a Major triad which is a minor seventh above the root. The dominant seventh chord has four different notes.

| D MAJOR TRIAD | MINOR 7TH | D DOMINANT 7TH CHORD |

The dominant seventh is so named because it is based on the $V$ or dominant chord, and has the interval of a 7th within the chord.

To write dominant seventh chords within a given key, find the fifth note of the key, and write a $V$ chord. Then, add the note which is a minor 7th above the <u>root</u> of the chord. When in harmonic minor, the third of the chord (which is the leading tone or 7th note of the key) must be raised a half-step.

Inversions of the dominant seventh are:

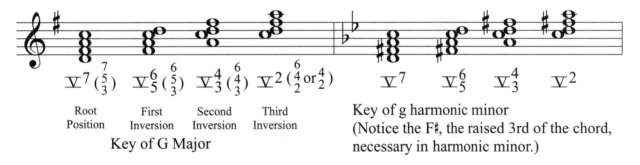

$$V^7 \left(^5_3\right) \qquad V^6_5 \left(^6_3\right) \qquad V^4_3 \left(^6_4\right) \qquad V^2 \left(^6_4 \text{ or } ^4_2\right)$$

| Root Position | First Inversion | Second Inversion | Third Inversion |

Key of G Major

$$V^7 \qquad V^6_5 \qquad V^4_3 \qquad V^2$$

Key of g harmonic minor
(Notice the F♯, the raised 3rd of the chord, necessary in harmonic minor.)

Dominant seventh chords can be on a given note, or in a given key. When asked to write a dominant seventh on a given note, write a Major triad with an added minor seventh.

When asked to write a dominant seventh in a given key, find the $V$ chord for the key, and add a note which is a minor seventh above the root. In Major keys, no accidentals will be added to the chord. In minor keys, the third will be raised because of harmonic minor.

**Dominant 7th on D**                    **Dominant 7th in the key of D Major**

42

1. Write dominant seventh chords and their inversions in the following keys, and label the chords with Roman numerals and figured bass. Remember to use harmonic minor. The first one is given.

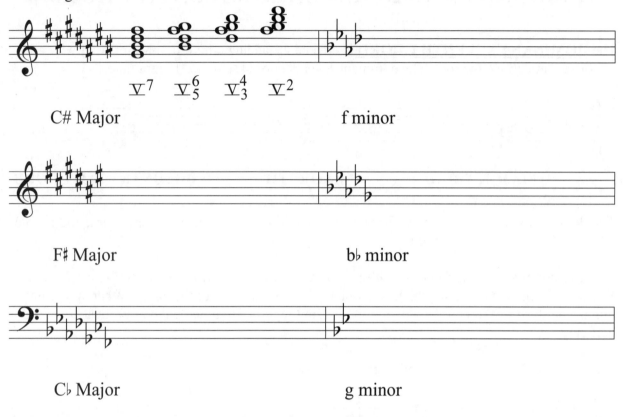

C# Major                                           f minor

F♯ Major                                           b♭ minor

C♭ Major                                           g minor

2. Complete dominant 7th chords and their inversions on these notes.

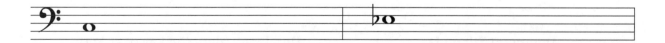

The **DIMINISHED SEVENTH CHORD** consists of a diminished triad, with the interval of a diminished seventh added to the top.

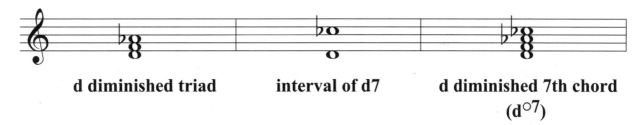

**d diminished triad**  **interval of d7**  **d diminished 7th chord**
**(d°7)**

Inversions of the diminished 7th chord are as follows:

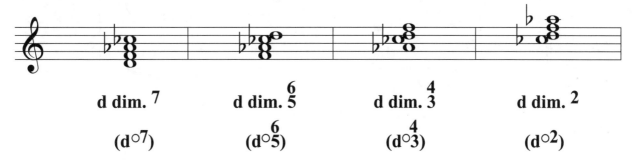

**d dim.** 7  **d dim.** 6 5  **d dim.** 4 3  **d dim.** 2

**(d°7)**  **(d°6 5)**  **(d°4 3)**  **(d°2)**

3. Write these diminished 7th chords and their inversions. The first one is given.

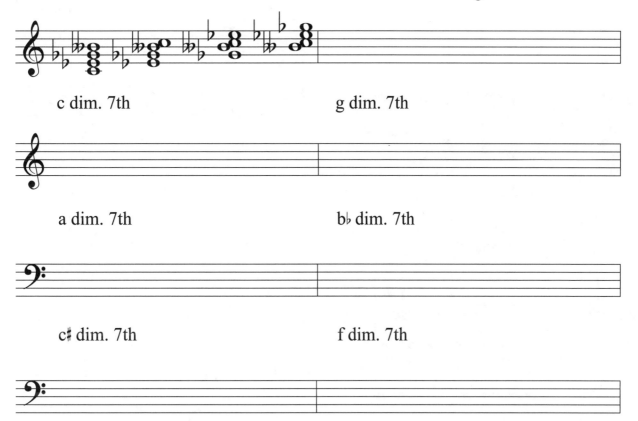

c dim. 7th  g dim. 7th

a dim. 7th  b♭ dim. 7th

c♯ dim. 7th  f dim. 7th

e♭ dim. 7th  f♯ dim. 7th

44

4. Label the boxed seventh chord in each example below. Some are dominant 7th chords, and some are diminished 7th chords. Label each dominant 7th chord with its Roman numeral and figured bass ($\underline{V}$7, $\underline{V}_5^6$, etc.). Label each diminished 7th chord with its root and figured bass (c dim. 7, c dim. $_5^6$, or c°7, c°$_5^6$, etc.).

a. Schumann: *May Sweet May*

b. Beethoven: *Sonata, Op. 49, No. 2*

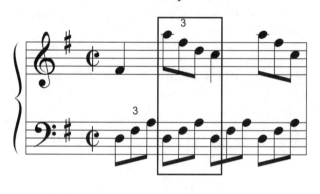

c. Mozart: *Sonata, K. 545*

d. Chopin: *Prelude, Op. 28, No. 4*

e. Chopin: *Prelude, Op. 28, No. 4*

f. Chopin: *Prelude, Op. 28, No. 4*

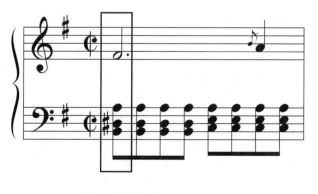

g. Untitled

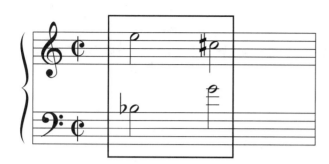

h. Chopin: *Prelude, Op. 28, No. 6*

i. Chopin: *Prelude, Op. 28, No. 6*

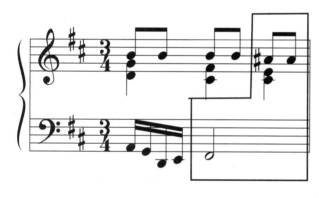

j. Schubert: *Scherzo, DV. 593*

k. Schubert: *Scherzo, DV. 593*

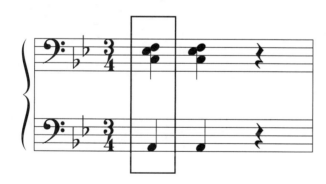

l. Schumann: *Knecht Ruppert*

46

m. Schumann: *Knecht Ruppert*

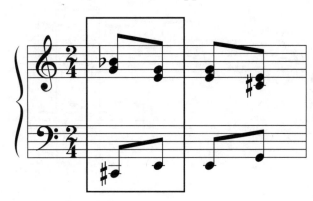

n. Schumann: *Knecht Ruppert*

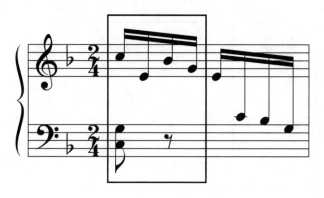

# LESSON 7
# AUTHENTIC, HALF, PLAGAL, AND DECEPTIVE CADENCES; CHORD PROGRESSIONS

A **CADENCE** is a closing or ending for a musical phrase, made up of a combination of chords. There are many types of cadences. Four common cadences are:

### AUTHENTIC, HALF, PLAGAL, and DECEPTIVE CADENCES

An **AUTHENTIC CADENCE** consists of a $\underline{V}$ or $\underline{V}^7$ chord followed by a I chord:

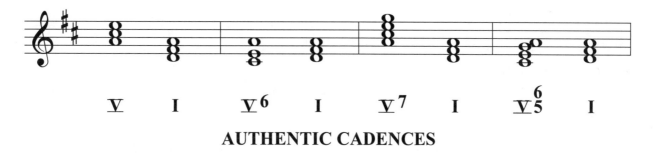

**AUTHENTIC CADENCES**

1. Write authentic cadences in these keys, using the chords indicated by the Roman Numerals. Determine whether to use the Major or minor key by the quality of the Roman Numerals. The first one is given.

48

A **PLAGAL CADENCE** consists of a IV chord followed by a I chord:

**PLAGAL CADENCES**

2. Write plagal cadences in these keys, using the chords indicated by the Roman Numerals. The first one is given.

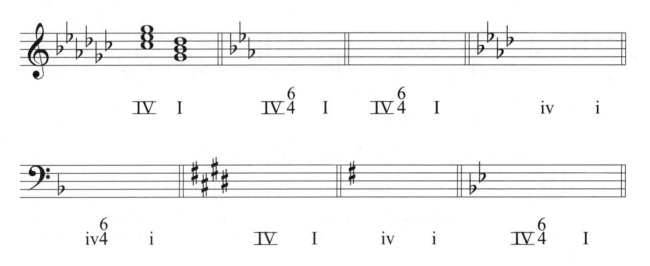

A **HALF CADENCE** is a cadence which ends with a V or V$^7$ chord:

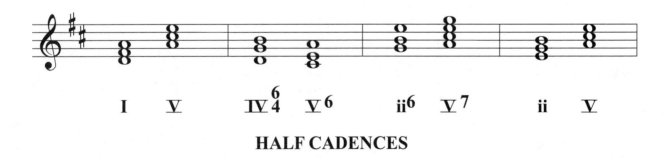

**HALF CADENCES**

3. Write half cadences in these keys, using the chords indicated by the Roman numerals. The first one is given. Remember to use harmonic minor.

$$\text{I} \quad \underline{\text{V}} \qquad \text{iv}^{6}_{4} \quad \underline{\text{V}}^{7} \qquad \text{ii}^{6} \quad \underline{\text{V}}^{7} \qquad\qquad \text{I} \quad \underline{\text{V}}$$

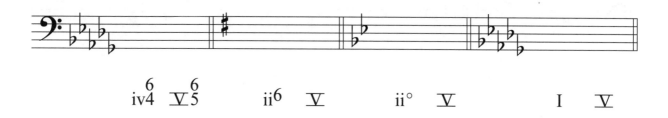

$$\text{iv}^{6}_{4} \quad \underline{\text{V}}^{6}_{5} \qquad \text{ii}^{6} \quad \underline{\text{V}} \qquad \text{ii}° \quad \underline{\text{V}} \qquad\qquad \text{I} \quad \underline{\text{V}}$$

A **DECEPTIVE CADENCE** consists of a $\underline{\text{V}}$ (or sometimes $\underline{\text{IV}}$) chord followed by a vi chord:

$$\underline{\text{V}} \qquad \text{vi} \qquad\qquad \underline{\text{IV}} \qquad \text{vi}$$

**DECEPTIVE CADENCES**

4. Write deceptive cadences in these keys, using the chords indicated by the Roman numerals. The first one is given.

5. Label the chords of each of these cadences with Roman numerals and figured bass, then write the name of the cadence (authentic, half, plagal, or deceptive) on the line below the Roman numerals. The first one is given.

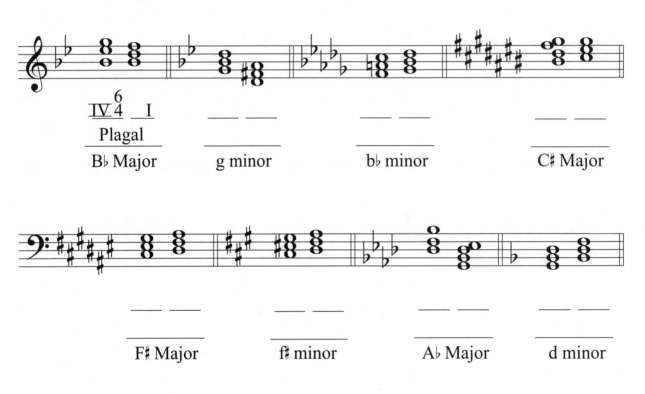

A **CHORD PROGRESSION** or **MIXED CADENCE** is created by combining certain chords from a given key, using positions for the chords that allow for a smooth transition from one chord to the next. The following are common chord progressions used in piano music:

Major keys:

Minor keys:

52

6. Write the following chord progressions. Determine whether to use the Major or minor key by the quality of the Roman numerals. The first one is given.

I    IV    ii    V⁷    I          i    iv    ii°    V    i

i    iv    ii°    V    i          I    IV    ii    V⁷    vi

I    IV    ii    V    vi          i    iv    ii°    V⁷    VI

i    iv    ii°    V⁷    VI          I    IV    ii    V    I

When naming cadences in music literature, label the last two chords of the phrase with their Roman numerals. These are the two chords which make up the cadence. Then, name the cadence (authentic, half, plagal, or deceptive).

Example (From *Sonata, Op. 49, no. 2,* by Beethoven):  Key of G Major, Authentic Cadence

$$\underline{V}7 \qquad I$$

7. Name the Major or minor key for each of the following examples. Label each underlined chord with its Roman numeral and figured bass, then name the cadence.

a. From *Sonatina, Hob. XVI:4*, by Haydn.

Key of: _____

Type of Cadence: _____

b. From *Sonatina, Op. 20, No. 2,* by Kuhlau.

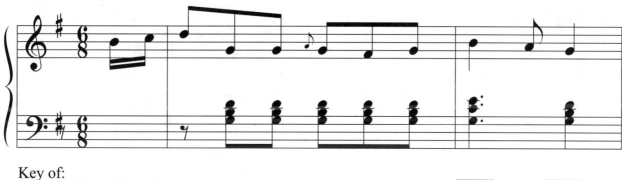

Key of: _____

Type of Cadence: _____

c. From *Sonata, K. 545,* by Mozart.

Key of: _____

Type of Cadence: _____     ____ ____

d. From *Prelude, Op. 28, No. 6,* by Chopin.

Key of: _____

Type of Cadence: _____     ____ ____

e. From *Album for the Young, Op. 68, No. 26*, by Schumann.

Key of: _____

Type of Cadence: _____     ____ ____

f. From *Prelude, Op. 28, No. 6,* by Chopin.

Key of: _____ _____ _____

Type of Cadence: _____

g. From *Prelude, Op. 28, No. 4,* by Chopin.

Key of: _____ _____ _____

Type of Cadence: _____

h. From *Sonata, Op. 49, No. 2,* by Beethoven.

Key of: _____ _____ _____

Type of Cadence: _____

i. From *Sheherazade*, by Schumann.

Key of: _____

Type of Cadence: _____

j. From *Prelude, Op. 28, No. 4,* by Chopin.

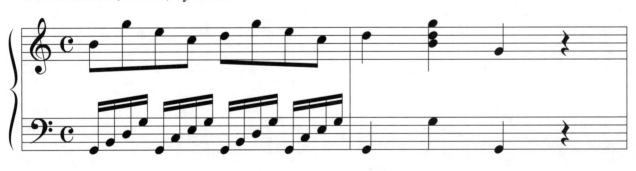

Key of: _____

Type of Cadence: _____

k. From *Sonata, K. 545,* by Mozart.

Key of: _____

Type of Cadence: _____

# REVIEW
## TERMS USED IN LESSONS 1-7

**Aeolian mode:** scale or tonality with the same pattern of half steps and whole steps that occur when beginning and ending on the sixth note of the Major scale, like natural minor; half steps occur between notes 2-3 and 5-6, as if playing all white keys from A to A

**authentic cadence**: a $V$-I cadence; in harmomic minor, $V$-i

**cadence**: a closing or ending for a phrase of music, made up of two or more chords

**chromatic scale:** a scale consisting of all twelve notes, with half-steps between all notes

**deceptive cadence:** a $V$-vi cadence; in harmonic minor, $V$ - $VI$

**diminished seventh chord:** a four note chord made up of a diminished triad and a diminished 7th above the root

**dominant seventh**: a four note chord made up of a Major triad and a minor 7th above the root; root position is $V^7$, first inversion is $V\,^6_5$, second inversion is $V\,^4_3$, and third inversion is $V^2$

**Dorian mode:** scale or tonality with the same pattern of half steps and whole steps that occur when beginning and ending on the second note of the Major scale; half steps occur between notes 2-3 and 6-7, as if playing all white keys from D to D

**first inversion**: a triad written with the third as the lowest note

**half cadence**: a cadence which ends with the $V$ chord

**interval**: the distance between two notes, named with numbers

**inversion**: a triad with a note other than the root as the lowest note

**Ionian mode:** scale or tonality with the same pattern of half steps and whole steps as the Major scale; half steps occur between notes 3-4 and 7-8, like the major scale

**key signature:** the sharps or flats at the beginning of a composition that indicate the key or tonality and which notes receive sharps or flats

**Mixolydian mode:** scale with the same pattern of half steps and whole steps that occur when beginning and ending on the fifth note of the Major scale; half steps occur between notes 3-4 and 6-7, as if playing all white keys from G to G

**modes:** scales or tonalities

58

**plagal cadence**: a IV-I cadence; in minor, iv-i

**primary triads**: the I, IV, and V chords; in minor, i, iv, and V

**root position**: a triad written in a position so that the note which names it is lowest

**scale**: a series of notes in alphabetical order (for example, C-D-E-F-G-A-B-C) with a specific pattern of whole steps and half steps

**scale degree names**: tonic (I), supertonic (ii), mediant (iii), subdominant (IV), dominant (V), submediant (vi), leading tone (vii°)

**second inversion**: a triad written with the fifth as the lowest note

**secondary triads**: the ii, iii, vi, and vii° chords; in minor, ii , III$^+$/III, VI, and vii°

**triad:** a chord with three different notes based on the interval of a third; qualities may be Major, minor, Augmented, or diminished.

**whole tone scale:** a scale that consists entirely of whole steps.

# REVIEW
## LESSONS 1-7

1. Name these Major keys.

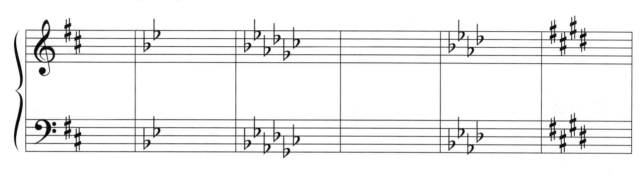

_____   _____   _____   _____   _____   _____

2. Name these minor keys.

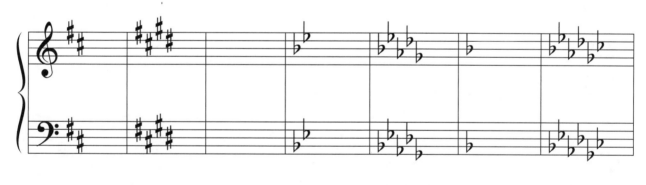

_____   _____   _____   _____   _____   _____   _____

3. Write the key signatures for these keys in both clefs.

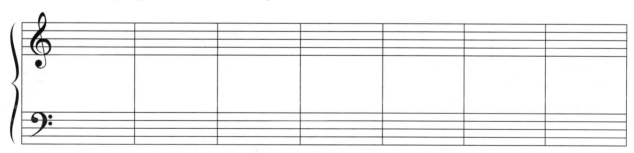

e minor      G Major      E♭ Major      f♯ minor      A Major      D♭ Major      a♭ minor

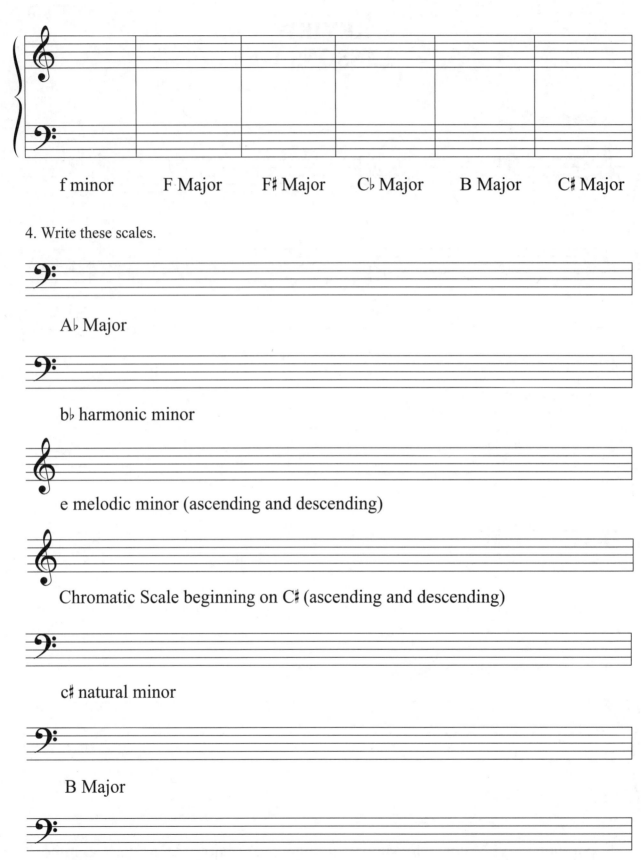

f minor       F Major       F♯ Major       C♭ Major       B Major       C♯ Major

4. Write these scales.

A♭ Major

b♭ harmonic minor

e melodic minor (ascending and descending)

Chromatic Scale beginning on C♯ (ascending and descending)

c♯ natural minor

B Major

Mixolydian mode beginning on G

eb harmonic minor

g# melodic minor, ascending and descending

Whole tone beginning on F

5. Label these chords with their roots (letter names), qualities (Major, minor, Augmented, diminished, dominant 7th, or diminished 7th), and figured bass.

6. Write these chords.

c# dim. $^6_4$   d dim. $^6_5$   bb dim.   Ab $^4_3$   cb min.$^6$   B Aug. $^6_4$

gb min.   eb min. $^6_4$   e dim. $^4_3$   f min.$^6$   Bb$^2$   a dim.

62

7. Name these intervals.

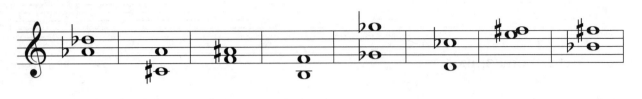

_____  _____  _____  _____  _____  _____  _____  _____

8. Complete these intervals. Do not change the given note.

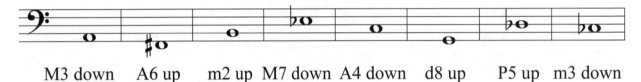

M3 down    A6 up    m2 up   M7 down   A4 down   d8 up    P5 up   m3 down

9. Name the Major key to which each of these dominant sevenths belongs.

_____  _____  _____  _____  _____  _____  _____

10. Write the scale degree names for the following Roman numerals.

a. I or i _____

b. ii or ii° _____

c. iii or III⁺/III _____

d. IV or iv _____

e. V _____

f. vi or VI _____

g. vii _____

11. Write the Roman numerals for the following cadences, and name each cadence.

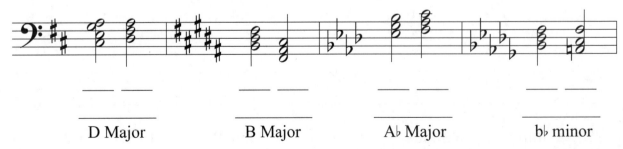

___ ___         ___ ___         ___ ___         ___ ___

___            ___            ___            ___

D Major         B Major        A♭ Major        b♭ minor

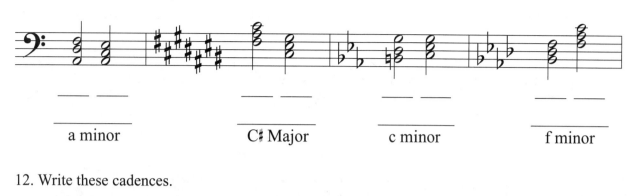

a minor    C# Major    c minor    f minor

12. Write these cadences.

V    vi        iv $\frac{6}{4}$    i        I    V    V$^6$    i

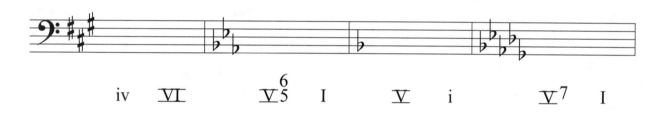

iv    VI        V$\frac{6}{5}$    I        V    i        V$^7$    I

13. Write the following chord progressions.

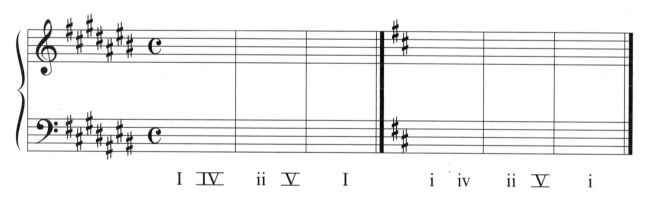

I    IV    ii    V    I        i    iv    ii    V    i

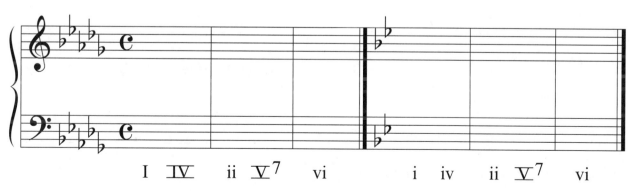

I    IV    ii    V$^7$    vi        i    iv    ii    V$^7$    vi

14. The following example is from *Sonata, Op. 49, No. 2*, by Beethoven. Answer the questions about the music.

a. What is the key or tonality? _____ _____

b. What type of scale is used on the last two beats of the final measure? _____

c. Name each boxed chord with its root, quality, Roman numeral, and figured bass. The first one is given.

|  | ROOT | QUALITY | ROMAN NUMERAL AND FIGURED BASS |
|---|---|---|---|
| Triad 1 | G | Major | I |
| Triad 2 | | | |
| Triad 3 | | | |
| Triad 4 | | | |

d. Name each circled interval.

a. _____ b. _____ c. _____ d. _____ e. _____ f. _____

e. Name the cadence in measures 7-8. _____

15. The following example is from *Scherzo, DV 593*, by Schubert. Answer the questions about the music.

a. What is the key or tonality? _____ _____

b. Name each boxed chord with its root, quality, Roman numeral, and figured bass.

| | ROOT | QUALITY | ROMAN NUMERAL AND FIGURED BASS |
|---|---|---|---|
| Triad 1 | _____ | _____ | _____ |
| Triad 2 | _____ | _____ | _____ |
| Triad 3 | _____ | _____ | _____ |
| Triad 4 | _____ | _____ | _____ |

c. Name each circled interval.

a. _____   b. _____   c. _____   d. _____   e. _____   f. _____

d. Write the Roman numerals for the chords in measures 7-8 that make the final cadence.

Measure 7: _____     Measure 8: _____

What type of cadence is this? _____

16. The following example is from *Knecht Ruppert* by Schumann. Answer the questions about the music.

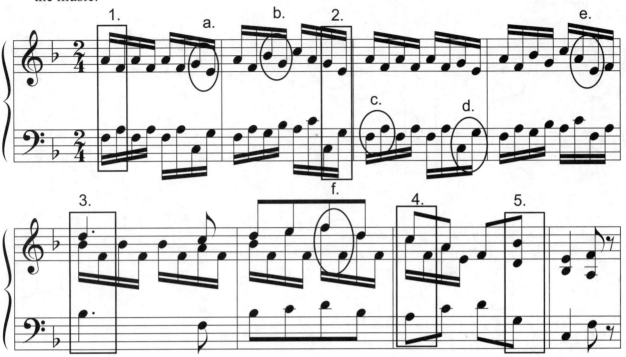

a. What is the key or tonality? _____ _____

b. This example is from the middle section of the music. The piece begins in the key of a minor. What is the Roman numeral for this section? _____

c. Name each boxed chord with its root, quality, Roman numeral, and figured bass.

|  | ROOT | QUALITY | ROMAN NUMERAL AND FIGURED BASS |
|---|---|---|---|
| Triad 1 | _____ | _____ | _____ |
| Triad 2 | _____ | _____ | _____ |
| Triad 3 | _____ | _____ | _____ |
| Triad 4 | _____ | _____ | _____ |
| Triad 5 | _____ | _____ | _____ |

d. Name each circled interval.

   a. _____    b. _____    c. _____    d. _____    e. _____    f. _____

e. What type of cadence used in measure 8? _____

# LESSON 8
# TIME SIGNATURES

The **TIME SIGNATURE** for a composition is found at the beginning, next to the key signature. The time signature is made up of two numbers:

Sometimes, the letter **C** or **₵** is used instead of numbers.

**C** stands for $\frac{4}{4}$, or **Common Time.**

**₵** stands for $\frac{2}{2}$, or **Alla Breve.**

The **top** number of the time signature tells **how many beats each measure contains.**

The **bottom** number tells **which type of note receives one beat.**

**2** = 2 beats per measure
**4** = Quarter note (♩) receives one beat

**3** = 3 beats per measure
**8** = Eighth note (♪) receives one beat

**METER** is determined by the time signature, and refers to the division of beats into equal groups, such as groups of three beats per measure in $\frac{3}{4}$ time.

68

When the bottom number of a time signature is a "4," a quarter note (♩) receives one beat. The following chart shows how many beats to give these notes or rests (other types of counting are possible):

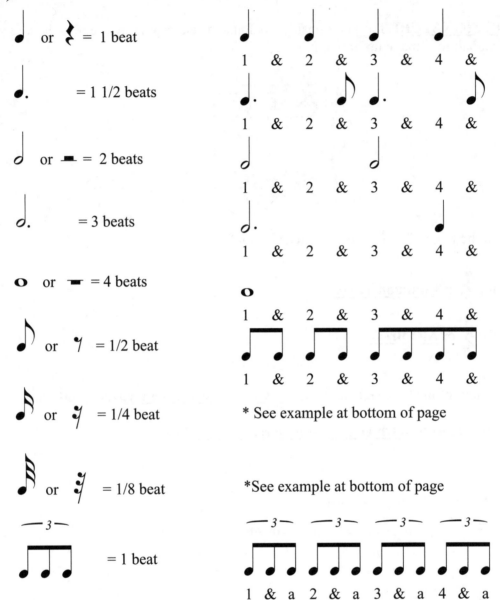

* Counting for some of the more common eighth, sixteenth, and thirty-second note patterns is shown here:

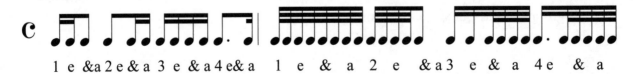

1 e &a 2 e &a 3 e &a 4 e& a     1 e & a 2 e &a 3 e & a 4e & a

An **UPBEAT** occurs when an incomplete measure begins the music. The last beat or beats are "borrowed" from the final measure and placed at the beginning. The beats used for the upbeat measure will be the last numbers of the time signature. The final measure will have fewer beats than normal. The first full measure begins with count number 1.

Example:

4 & 1 & 2 & 3 & 4 & 1 & 2 & 3 &

When the bottom number of a time signature is a "2," a half note (𝅗𝅥) receives one beat. The following chart shows how many beats to give these notes or rests (other types of counting are possible):

𝅗𝅥 or 𝄼 = 1 beat

𝅗𝅥. = 1 1/2 beats

𝅝 or 𝄻 = 2 beats

♩ or 𝄽 = 1/2 beat

♪ or 𝄾 = 1/4 beat

𝅘𝅥𝅮 or 𝄿 = 1/8 beat

𝅘𝅥𝅯 or 𝅀 = 1/16 beat

𝅗𝅥 𝅗𝅥
1 & 2 &

𝅗𝅥. ♩
1 & 2 &

𝅝
1 & 2 &

♩ ♩ ♩ ♩
1 & 2 &

♫ ♫ ♩ ♫
1 e & a 2 e & a

♬ ♬ ♬
1 e & a 2 e & a

[sixteenth note run]
1 e & a

70

When the time signature has an 8 on the bottom, an eighth note (♪) receives one beat. (Other types of counting are possible.)

♪ or 𝄾 = 1/2 beat

1 & 2 & 3 & 4 & 5 & 6 &

♪ or 𝄾 = 1 beat

1    2    3    4    5    6

♩ or 𝄽 = 2 beats

1    2    3    4    5    6

♩. or 𝄽 𝄾 = 3 beats

1    2    3    4    5    6

𝅗𝅥. or ■ = 6 beats

1    2    3    4    5    6

𝅝. = 12 beats

1 2 3 4 5 6 7 8 9 10 11 12

1. Fill in the blanks. The first one is given.

**2/4** = <u>2 beats per measure</u>
= <u>Quarter note receives one beat</u>

**3/4** = _____
= _____

**3/8** = _____
= _____

**¢** = _____
= _____

**C** = _____
= _____

**2/2** = _____
= _____

**7/4** = _____
= _____

**6/8** = _____
= _____

When a time signature has a 2 on top ( $\frac{2}{2}$, $\frac{2}{4}$, etc.), the first beat of the measure is strongest.

When a time signature has a 3 on top ( $\frac{3}{4}$, $\frac{3}{8}$, etc.), the first beat of the measure is strongest.

When a time signature has a 4 on top ( $\frac{4}{2}$, $\frac{4}{4}$, etc.), the first beat of the measure is strongest, and the third beat is also a strong beat.

When a time signature has a 6 on top ( $\frac{6}{4}$, $\frac{6}{8}$, etc.), the first beat of the measure is strongest, and the fourth beat is also a strong beat.

**Note**: The accents above are only intended to demonstrate where strong and weak beats occur within the given meter. They are not meant to imply that every strong beat receives an accent.

**SYNCOPATION** occurs when there is a disturbance of the normal pulse or meter, often created by a strong note on a weak beat. The syncopations are circled in the example below.

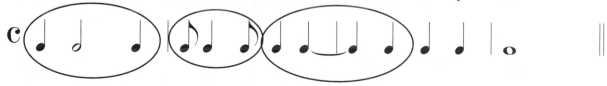

2. Write counts for these phrases, and place accents on the strong beats.

a. From *Sadness of Soul, Op. 53, No. 4,* by Mendelssohn.

b. From *Sonatina, Op. 55, No. 2,* by Kuhlau.

c. From *Mazurka, Op. 67, No. 2,* by Chopin.

d. From *Sonatina, Op. 20, No. 3*, by Kuhlau.

e. From *Prelude, Op. 28, No. 20,* by Chopin.

74

f. From *French Suite No. 5*, by J.S. Bach.

g. From *Mazurka, Op. 7, No. 1*, by Chopin.

h. From *Roundelay*, by Schumann.

# LESSON 9
# SIGNS AND TERMS

The following performance terms may appear in music you are studying.

*a tempo:* return to the original tempo

 **accent:** play the note louder than the others

*accelerando:* accelerate; gradually faster

**accidentals:** sharps, flats, or naturals written before the notes that are not in the key signature

*adagio:* slowly

*allargando:* broadening; gradually slower

*allegro:* fast or quick, cheerfully, merrily

*allegretto:* slighly slower than *allegro*; faster than *andante*

*andante:* a moderate walking tempo.

*andantino:* slightly faster than *andante;* some composers use it to mean slower than *andante*

*animato:* animated; with spirit

*appoggiatura:* used mainly in music of the Classical Period (see Lesson 14), play the first note as half the value of the second note*

*arpeggio:* a broken chord:

**atonality:** no specific key or tonality

**articulation:** the manner in which notes are executed, including but not limited to *legato* and *staccato*

**bitonality:** the use of two different keys at the same time

**canon:** a strict form of contrapuntal writing in which each voice exactly imitates the melody of the first voice

*cantabile:* in a singing style

* Interpretation of the *appoggiatura* depends on many factors. Further study is recommended.

*con brio:* with vigor or spirit (with brilliance)

*coda:* an extended ending

*codetta:* a short coda, or a short section of music that connects two other sections but is not part of either

*con:* with

*con moto:* with motion

 *crescendo (cresc.):* gradually louder

*D.C. al fine:* go back to the beginning and play to *fine*

𝄆 ❀ or |_____| **damper pedal:** press the pedal located on the right

 *decrescendo (decresc.) or diminuendo (dim.):* gradually softer

*dolce:* sweetly

*doloroso:* sadly; sorrowfully

**double flat:** two flats placed before a note, indicating to lower the note a whole step

B double flat is
the same pitch as A

**double sharp:** the symbol 𝄪 placed before a note, indicating to raise the note a whole step

G double sharp is
the same pitch as A

**dynamics:** letters or symbols that indicate how loudly or softly to play the music

**enharmonic:** two different names for the same pitch, such as C♯ and D♭

*espressivo:* expressively

*fine:* the end

*f*    **_forte:_** loud

*ff*    **_fortissimo:_** very loud

*fff*    **_fortississimo:_** very, very loud

*fp*    **_forte-piano:_** loud followed immediately by soft

⌢    **_fermata:_** hold the note longer than its value

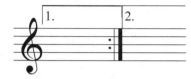 **first and second ending:** Play the music with the first ending (under the 1.), then repeat the music; the second time through, skip the first ending and play the second ending (under the 2.)

**_giocoso:_** merrily, with humor

**_gracioso:_** gracefully

**_largo:_** very slowly

**_legato:_** play smoothly; connect the notes

**_leggiero:_** lightly, delicately

**_lento:_** slowly

**_marcato:_** stressed, marked

**_meno:_** less

*mf*    **_mezzo forte:_** medium loud

*mp*    **_mezzo piano:_** medium soft

**_moderato:_** a moderate or medium tempo

**_molto:_** much; very

 **mordent:** an ornament in which the written note is played, followed by the note below the written note and the written note again:

 **octave Sign (8va):** play the notes an octave higher (or lower if below the notes) than where they are written.

**opus:** a word used to indicate the chronological order in which a composer's music was written

*ostinato:* a persistently repeated pattern, such as: 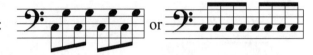 or

**parallel Major/minor:** Major and minor keys with the same letter names (such as C Major and c minor)

𝆏 *piano:* soft

𝆏𝆏 *pianissimo:* very soft

𝆏𝆏𝆏 *pianississimo:* very, very soft

*pesante:* heavily

**phrase:** a musical sentence, often but not always four measures long

*piu:* more

*piu mosso:* more motion; faster

*poco:* little

**polytonality:** the use of several different keys at the same time

*presto:* very fast

*rallentando (rall.):* gradually slower

**repeat sign:** repeat the previous sections of music; go back to the nearest repeat sign, or to the beginning if there is none

*ritardando (ritard., rit.,):* gradually slower

*ritenuto:* immediately slower

*robusto:* robustly, boldly

*scherzando:* playfully, jokingly

*sempre:* always

*senza:* without

**sf  fz  sfz**    *sforzando*: a sudden, sharp accent

*simile:* continue in the same style

 **slur:** curved line indicating to play *legato*

*spiritoso:* spirited; with spirit

*sostenuto:* sustained

 **staccato:** play crisply or detached

*subito:* suddenly; at once

*syncopation:* a momentary contradiction of the meter or pulse, often by changing strong and weak beats within a measure, for example:

**tempo:** the speed at which to play the music

 *tenuto:* hold the note for its full value; may also mean to stress the note

*tranquillo:* tranquilly, peacefully, calmly

*tre corda (t.c.):* release the *una corda* pedal (soft pedal; left pedal)

 **tie:** hold the second note; do not play it

*tranquillo:* tranquilly; peacefully; calmly

**trill:** An ornament in which the written note is alternated continuously with the note above. In music of the Baroque or Classical Period (see Lessons 13 and 14), begin the trill on the note above the written note (example A). In music of the Romantic Period (Lesson 15), begin on the written note (example B).*

Baroque or Classical Period: begin on the note above the written note.

Romantic Period: begin on the written note.

*The trill may be interpreted differently. Further study is recommended.

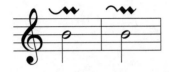

**trill with prefix:** a trill performed with an added beginning from above or below

**turn:** an ornament in which the written note is surrounded by its upper and lower neighbors:

*una corda (u.c.):* press the left or soft pedal

*vivace:* quick, lively

*vivo:* brisk, lively

*...etto:* a suffix meaning little or less than, such as *allegretto* for a little slower than *allegro*

*...ino:* a suffix meaning little or less than, such as *andantino* for a little faster than *andante*

1. Match these terms and symbols with their definitions.

_____ *ppp*

_____ *mf*

_____ 8*va*

_____ *sfz  sf  fz*

_____ *ff*

_____ *fff*

_____ dynamics

_____ *p*

_____ *mp*

_____ *f*

_____ *pp*

a. *mezzo piano:* medium soft

b. *pianissimo:* very soft

c. *piano:* soft

d. *fortissimo:* very loud

e. *mezzo forte:* medium loud

f. symbols that indicate loud or soft

g. *forte:* loud

h. play one octave higher

i. *fortississimo:* very, very loud

j. *sforzando:* a sudden, sharp accent

k. *pianississimo:* very, very soft

2. Match these terms and symbols with their definitions.

_____ legato

a. slur: curved line to indicate *legato*

b. repeat sign: repeat the music

c. *staccato:* crisply or detached

d. play smoothly or connected

e. fermata: hold the note longer than its value

f. first and second endings

3. Match these terms and symbols with their definitions.

_____ 

_____ 𝓟𝑒𝑑. ❋ |_____|

_____ phrase

_____ 

_____ D. C. al fine

_____ ritardando (rit.)

_____ a tempo

a. press the damper pedal (the pedal on the right)

b. a musical sentence, often but not always four measures long

c. *tenuto:* hold the note for its full value; may also mean to stress the note

d. accent: play the note louder than the others

e. gradually slower

f. return to the original tempo

g. go back to the beginning and play to the word *fine*

4. Match these terms and symbols with their definitions.

_____ *allegro*          a. walking tempo

_____ *andante*          b. gradually louder

_____ *moderato*         c. gradually slower

_____ *vivace*           d. gradually softer

_____ ⟍⟋          e. slowly

_____ ⟋⟍          f. a moderate or medium tempo

_____ *adagio*           g. quick or lively

_____ *lento*            h. with brilliance

_____ *rallentando (rall.)*   i. fast, quick, cheerfully, merrily

_____ *con brio*         j. slowly

5. Match these terms and symbols with their definitions.

_____ *fp*               a. sadly, sorrowfully

_____ *scherzando*       b. boldly, robustly

_____ *doloroso*         c. more

_____ opus               d. heavily

_____ *robusto*          e. sustained

_____ *piu*              f. playfully, jokingly

_____ *pesante*          g. system of classifying a composer's works chronologically

_____ *sostenuto*        h. loud, followed immediately by soft

6. Match these terms and symbols with their definitions.

_____ *andantino*

_____ *con moto*

_____ *dolce*

_____

_____ *accelerando*

_____

_____ *una corda*

_____ *cantabile*

_____ *molto*

_____

_____

_____ *codetta*

_____ *poco*

_____ *tre corde*

_____ *spiritoso*

_____

_____ *coda*

_____ *sempre*

_____

a. trill:

b. gradually faster

c. trill with prefix:

d. use soft pedal (left pedal)

e. slightly faster than *andante*

f. sweetly

g. with motion

h. with spirit

i. little

j. much, greatly

k. a short coda, or a short section of music that connects two other sections but is not part or either

l. release the soft pedal (left pedal)

m. trill with prefix:

n. in a singing style

o. mordent:

p. an extended ending

q. *appoggiatura:*

r. always

s. turn:

7. Match these terms with their definitions.

| | | |
|---|---|---|
| _____ | *presto* | a. expressively |
| _____ | *vivo* | b. without |
| _____ | *espressivo* | c. suddenly; at once |
| _____ | *leggiero* | d. very fast |
| _____ | *senza* | e. stressed; marked |
| _____ | *marcato* | f. brisk, lively |
| _____ | *subito* | g. continue in the same style |
| _____ | *simile* | h. lightly; delicately |
| _____ | double sharp | i. a repeated pattern |
| _____ | *ostinato* | j. two flats before a note |
| _____ | *arpeggio* | k. an ✕ before a note |
| _____ | double flat | l. a broken chord |

8. Match these terms with their definitions.

| | | |
|---|---|---|
| _____ | *largo* | a. animated; with spirit |
| _____ | *giocoso* | b. gracefully |
| _____ | *animato* | c. with fire |
| _____ | bitonality | d. no specific key or tonality |
| _____ | *allegretto* | e. peacefully, calmly, tranquilly |
| _____ | *grazioso* | f. merrily, with humor |
| _____ | *con fuoco* | g. the use of two different keys at the same time |
| _____ | atonality | h. slightly slower than *allegro* |
| _____ | polytonality | i. very slowly |
| _____ | *tranquillo* | j. the use of several different keys at the same time |

85

86

9. Match these terms with their definitions.

_____ *allargando*

_____ *...etto*

_____ *...ino*

_____ *meno*

_____ canon

_____ *ritenuto*

_____ enharmonic

_____ parallel Major and minor

_____ relative Major and minor

_____ *meno mosso*

_____ *piu mosso*

_____ syncopation

_____ accidental

_____ articulation

a. two names for the same pitch

b. broadening, gradually slower

c. little

d. less motion

e. less

f. strong notes on weak beats

g. Major and minor keys with the same key signature

h. immediately slower

i. little

j. a strict form of contrapuntal writing in which each voice exactly imitates the melody of the first voice

k. more motion

l. Major and minor keys with the same letter names

m. the manner in which notes are executed, including but not limited to *staccato* and *legato*

n. sharp, flat, or natural written before the note (not in the key signature)

# LESSON 10
# COMPOSITIONAL TECHNIQUES

A **MOTIVE** is a short musical statement. The composer uses this motive as the main idea of the music and repeats it in many different ways.

A **THEME** is an entire phrase of music, which is the basis of the composition. (A composition may have more than one theme.)

This *Etude* by Couppey uses this **motive:**

It is repeated, with variations, several times at the beginning and throughout the music:

**REPETITION** takes place when the motive is repeated immediately, exactly the way it was the first time it occurred, on the same note.

*Clouds* by Mendelssohn uses repetition.

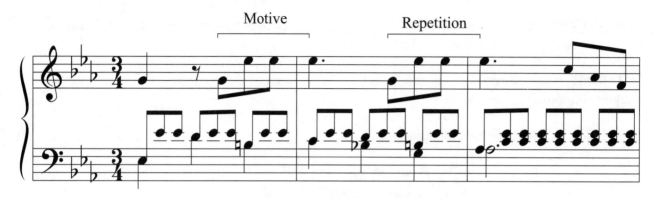

**SEQUENCE** occurs when the motive is repeated immediately, on a different note, usually a 2nd or 3rd higher or lower.

*Invention No. 1* by J.S. Bach uses sequence.

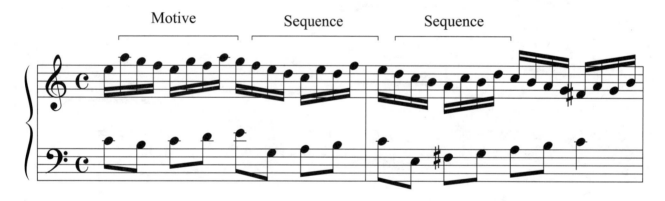

**IMITATION** occurs when the motive is repeated immediately in another voice, such as in the bass clef following a statement of the motive in the treble clef.

*Invention No. 3* by J.S. Bach uses imitation.

**CANON**\* occurs when the entire melody is repeated in another voice. The difference between imitation and canon is that imitation uses only a motive, while canon is a <u>strict copy of the entire melody.</u>

*Dona Nobis Pacem* shows the use of canon. Notice how the bass clef part copies the entire theme which was introduced in the treble clef.

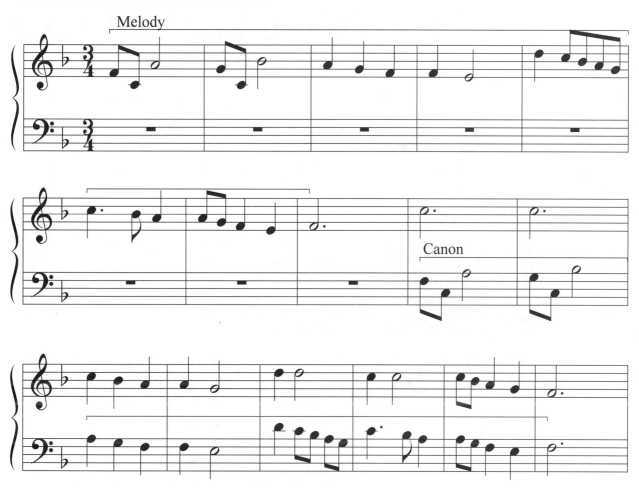

\*The term *canon* is used in a variety of ways when applied to music. Further study is recommended.

1. Circle the repetition, imitation, sequence, or canon in each example below, then write the type of technique on the line above the music.

a. From *Etude, Op. 24, No. 10,* by Couppey. _____

b. From *Slumber Song* by Gurlitt. _____

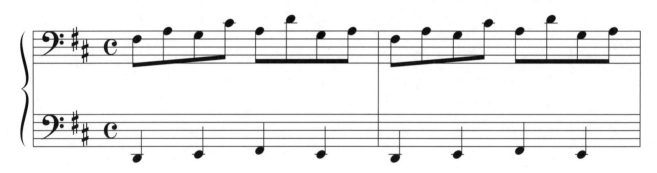

c. From *White Coral Bells* (folk song). _____

d. From *Russian Song, Op. 39, No. 11,* by Tchaikovsky. _____

e. From *Waltz, Op. 12, No. 2,* by Grieg. _____

f. From *Sweet Remembrance, Op. 19, No. 1*, by Mendelssohn. _____

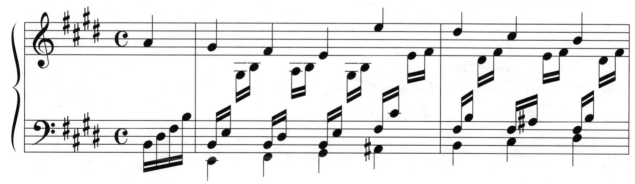

92

g. From Little Prelude No. 5 by J.S. Bach. _____

h. From *Alleluia* (anonymous). _____

# LESSON 11
# TRANSPOSITION

**TRANSPOSITION** occurs when a composition is played or written in a key that is different from the original.

For example, the first version of "Frere Jacques" below (Example A) is in the key of C Major. The second version (Example B) is in G Major. The music has been transposed from C Major to G Major.

Notice how the intervals remain the same in both versions, and if played, the melody sounds the same, but higher in pitch.

**EXAMPLE A:  FRERE JACQUES in the key of C Major**

**EXAMPLE B:  FRERE JACQUES  in the key of G Major**

Follow these steps when transposing a melody:

1. Determine the key of the original melody.

2. Determine the key signature of the key to which the music will be transposed.

3. Look at the first note of the original melody and determine its scale degree or its place in the scale. For example, if the original key is C Major and the melody begins on G, the  starting note is the 5th.

4. The first note for the new key will be the same interval above the new tonic as the original. For  example, when the new key is D Major and the starting note was a 5th above tonic, the new starting note will be A, a 5th above D.

5. Continue writing the transposition by determining each interval of the original melody and using that interval for the new melody. Add any necessary sharps or flats.

6. Check your progress by following steps 3 and 4 for any given note.

Example: Mary Had a Little Lamb, transposed from C Major to G Major.

1. Original key:  C Major.

2. New key signature for G Major:  F♯.

3. First note of original is E, the 3rd note of G Major

4. Starting note will be B, the 3rd note of G Major.

5. Melody moves up and down by seconds and thirds. See examples below.


## MARY HAD A LITTLE LAMB in C Major

## MARY HAD A LITTLE LAMB in G Major

Another way to transpose a melody is to move each note up or down the same distance. In the example of "Mary Had a Little Lamb" above, each note would be raised a Perfect 5th. The first E becomes B, the D becomes A, the C becomes G, etc.

1. Transpose this example (from *Ecossaise in G* by Beethoven) to the key of D Major. Write the transposition on the blank staff below the example.

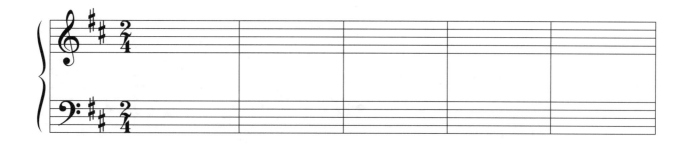

2. Transpose this example (from *Minuet in F* by Mozart) to the key of Bb Major. Write the transposition on the blank staff below the music.

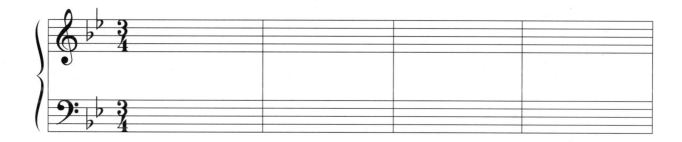

3. The example below has been transposed from e minor to c minor. The transposition has three incorrect notes. Find and circle each error.

# LESSON 12
# MODULATION

**MODULATION** occurs when a musical composition changes from the original key to another key, or changes tonal center, then remains in the new key for a reasonable amount of time.

Music may modulate to any other key, but frequently either the Dominant key ( $\underline{V}$ ) or the relative Major or minor is used.

In the example below, from *Little Prelude No. 2* by J.S. Bach, the music begins in the key of c minor and modulates to the key of E♭ Major (the relative Major).

Two important 20th Century theorists, Schoenberg and Schenker, taught that music does not truly modulate. Further study of Schenkerian Analysis is recommended.

1. Name the key to which each of these examples modulates.

a. From *Sonata in E♭* by Haydn. Original key: g minor     Modulates to: _____
   (Slightly edited to save space.)

b. From *Sonata No. 2* by Haydn. Original key: E♭ Major     Modulates to: _____

c. From *Sonata, K. 283: Andante* by Mozart. Original key: C Major     Modulates to: _____

# LESSON 13
# THE FOUR PERIODS OF MUSIC HISTORY
# THE BAROQUE PERIOD; FRESCOBALDI AND SOLER

The history of music since 1600 is divided into four periods (dates are approximate):

| | |
|---|---|
| **Baroque:** | **1600-1750** |
| **Classical:** | **1750-1830** |
| **Romantic:** | **1830-1900** |

**20th & 21st Centuries:   1900-present**
(Currently, there is not a definitive name for stylistic periods of the 20th and 21st Centuries. It is sometimes called the "Contemporary Period," "Modern," or "Post-Common Practice." It may also be divided into two groups: the 20th Century (1900-1999), and the Contemporary Period (2000-Present).

Music of the **BAROQUE PERIOD** (1600-1750) is characterized by the following:

a. **Polyphonic Texture:** Two or more separate voices are interchanged to create the music. The melodies are passed between the parts, and the parts are of equal importance.

b. **Use of Ornamentation:** Composers included many trills, mordents, and other ornaments in their music. It was the performer's responsibility to know how to play the ornaments correctly. Performers could also add their own ornaments at appropriate places in the music.

c. **Improvisation:** Not only did music of the Baroque Period contain many ornaments, the performer was also free to improvise sections of the music. This not only included adding the ornaments mentioned above, but also playing **Cadenzas**, entire sections of music that the performer created, often after a cadence in the music.

Another type of improvisation in Baroque music included the use of **Figured Bass.** The performer was given an outline of the chord progression of a composition. The performer improvised using the harmonies specified by the figured bass.

**FIGURED BASS**

d. Most keyboard music of the Baroque Period was written for the **harpsichord, clavichord**, and **organ**. The piano was not invented until fairly late in the Baroque Period. (The piano was invented sometime around 1700 by Bartolomeo Cristofori, but did not gain widespread use until several years later.)

e. **Terraced Dynamics:** Since much of the keyboard music from the Baroque Period was written for the harpsichord, which does not have the capability of making *crescendos* or *diminuendos*, performers used terraced dynamics. This takes place when the dynamics increase or decrease by sections: *p mp mf f*, rather than gradually. (This type of dynamic contrast was most prevelant in keyboard music. Other instruments, such as the violin, did create true *crescendos* and *decrescendos* during the Baroque Period.)

This example, from *Short Prelude No. 7* by J.S. Bach, shows these characteristics: Polyphonic texture and terraced dynamics.

## GIROLAMO FRESCOBALDI

**Girolamo Frescobaldi** lived during the Baroque Period. He was born in 1583, in Italy.

He was considered one of the greatest organists and keyboard composers of his time. He

held a number of positions during his lifetime, including organist of St. Maria in Trastevere,

organist of St. Peter's in Brussels, and organist at the Florentine court of Ferdinando II de'

Medici.

He wrote a variety of works, including keyboard fantasias, toccatas, and partitas. Two of

his more well known works are *Arie musicali* (1630), and *Fiori musicali* (1635) for use in

the Mass. These later works show great skill in contrapuntal writing, the most prevelant

type of writing in the Baroque Period.

Frescobaldi died in 1643 in Rome, but sixty years later J.S. Bach copied and studied his

music, acknowledging the contribution of Frescobaldi to music of the Baroque Period.

# ANTONIO SOLER

**Antonio Soler** was born in 1729, in Spain. He represents the late Baroque and early Classical Periods, but is generally considered a Baroque composer due to his compositional style.

As a child, Soler studied at the choir school at Montserrat. In 1752, he became a Jeronymite monk, and eventually took the position as music director at the monastery. While there, he studied with Domenico Scarlatti.

One of Soler's greatest contributions to music is not a composition, but instead is a theoretical book, *Llave de la modulacion* (1762) *(Key to Modulation and Musical Antiquities)*. In this work, Soler showed how to move from any Major or minor key to any other within moments. Although these concepts are completely acceptable today, in Soler's time it caused quite a controversy.

His keyboard works include many sonatas, first published in London in 1796. These sonatas show the influence of his purely Baroque teacher, Scarlatti, but also contain characteristics of music from the upcoming Classical Period (see Lesson 14), such as Alberti Bass.

Soler also wrote many sacred vocal works, and instrumental pieces. He was a scholarly writer as well, and wrote many books on music and its history. Unfortunately, much of his writing is now lost. He died in 1783.

Five other well known Baroque composers are:

**J.S. Bach**, born in Germany, 1685-1750

**G.F. Handel,** born in Germany, 1685-1760

**Domenico Scarlatti,** born in Italy, 1685-1757

**Henry Purcell,** born in England, 1659-1695

**Georg Philipp Telemann,** born in Germany, 1681-1767

1. Name the four periods of music history and give their dates.

_____  _____

_____  _____

_____  _____

_____  _____

2. List five characteristics of Baroque music and describe each.

a. _____

_____

_____

b. _____

_____

_____

c. _____

_____

_____

d. _____

_____

_____

e. _____

_____

_____

3. Complete the following information about each of these composers.

**Girolamo Frescobaldi**

Dates of birth and death: _____

Historical period: _____

Country of birth: _____

Primary instrument: _____

Positions held: _____

_____

_____

Keyboard works: _____

Other works: _____

Other contributions to music: _____

_____

**Antonio Soler**

Dates of birth and death: _____

Historical period: _____

Country of birth: _____

Positions held: _____

_____

Keyboard works: _____

Scholarly writings (with descriptions of contents): _____

_____

Other works: _____

_____

Influenced by whom and what: _____

_____

4. Name five other Baroque composers, their places of birth, and their dates of birth and death.

| | | |
|---|---|---|
| _____ | _____ | _____ |
| _____ | _____ | _____ |
| _____ | _____ | _____ |
| _____ | _____ | _____ |
| _____ | _____ | _____ |

# LESSON 14
# THE CLASSICAL PERIOD
# HAYDN AND BEETHOVEN

The **CLASSICAL PERIOD** of music took place from approximately 1750-1830. Music from the Classical Period includes the following characteristics:

a. **Homophonic Texture:** Much of the music of the Classical Period has an obvious melody.

b. **Harmonic structure easily recognizable:** Quite often, the harmony of a piece from the Classical Period is easy to hear, uncluttered by extra notes.

c. **Rests:** Before a new theme or sections is introduced, rests are often used to set off the new section.

d. **Alberti Bass:** A common type of accompaniment for the left hand part of piano music from the Classical Period is Alberti Bass, a broken chord accompaniment with the specific pattern of low - high - middle - high.

## ALBERTI BASS

e. **Sonata and Sonatina forms:** A sonata or sonatina may contain several movements (usually two, three, or four), with the first movement having an **Exposition, Development**, and **Recapitulation.** When there are three movements, the second is usually a slow movement in a different but related key, and the third is often a Rondo (ABACABA form), in the same key as the first movement.

| **Sonata Form:** | **Exposition** | **Development** | **Recapitulation** |
|---|---|---|---|
| (or Sonata Allegro Form) | Theme 1/Theme 2 Tonic   New Key | Use of themes in various keys | Theme1/Theme2 Tonic   Tonic |

This example, from *Sonatina, Op. 36, No. 3* by Clementi, shows these characteristics: Homophonic texture, clear melody and harmony, and use of rests.

# FRANZ JOSEF HAYDN

**Franz Josef Haydn** lived during the Classical Period of music history. He was born in Austria, near the Hungarian border, but studied music (as a choirboy) in Vienna from age 8. From his childhood. Haydn loved practical jokes.

After leaving the Vienna school (in his late teens), he wrote a great deal of music, and was hired as full time Director of Music to Prince Esterhazy at Eisenstadt. Haydn had a good salary, and had the opportunity to compose and have his music performed often. He was one of the first composers to begin developing Sonata form (Sonata Allegro form).

His love of practical jokes can be heard in his music. His *Farewell Symphony* was written at a time when the court musicians were overdue for a vacation. To remind Prince Esterhazy of this, Haydn arranged the music so that each musician leaves the stage when his part is over. By the end of the symphony, there are only two musicians left on stage.

In his *Surprise Symphony*, the second movement (the slow movement) has a carefully placed sudden *sforzando* after a quiet opening, to wake the audience.

Haydn wrote over 100 symphonies, giving him the nickname "Father of the Symphony," or "Papa Haydn." He developed the standard four movement format for a symphony. He also wrote chamber music, many piano sonatas, and varied works for other instruments and choir. Haydn died in 1809.

# LUDWIG VAN BEETHOVEN

**Ludwig van Beethoven** was born in Bonn, Germany in 1770, and is probably the most famous of all composers. He spent most of his life in Vienna, Austria, and made his living as a teacher and composer. Tragedy struck his life when he lost his hearing around age 30. Despite this, he continued composing, and some of his greatest works were written after he went deaf.

Beethoven wrote many works for piano, orchestra, and solo instruments. Although he usually is  considered a Classical composer, his music represents the transition between the Classical and Romantic periods. He wrote using Classical forms, but gave them new depth. His use of Sonata form shows this change, and he used richer harmonies and more complex rhythms. His nine symphonies also exhibit a grander use of the orchestra, paving the way for the Romantic Period.

Beethoven wrote 32 piano sonatas, five piano concertos, nine symphonies, and an abundance of other music, which includes several string quartets, choral music, and an opera. Beethoven died in 1827.


Other composers of the Classical period include:

**W.A. Mozart,** born in Austria, 1756-1791

**Muzio Clementi,** born in Italy, 1752-1832

**Frederich Kuhlau,** born in Germany, 1786-1832

**Carl Czerny,** born in Austria, 1791-1857

1. List five characteristics of music from the Classical Period and describe each.

a. _____

_____

_____

b. _____

_____

_____

c. _____

_____

_____

d. _____

_____

_____

e. _____

_____

_____

2. Complete the following information about each of these composers.

**Franz Josef Haydn**

Dates of birth and death: _____

Historical period: _____

Country of birth: _____

Education: _____

Position held: _____

_____

Major contributions to musical style: _____

_____

Types of compositions: _____

_____

Practical jokes in music: _____

_____

_____

## Ludwig von Beethoven

Dates of birth and death: _____

Historical period: _____

Country of birth: _____

Position held: _____

_____

_____

Types of compositions: _____

_____

Contributions to musical style: _____

_____

3. Name four other Classical composers, their places of birth, and their dates of birth and death.

_____   _____   _____

_____   _____   _____

_____   _____   _____

_____   _____   _____

4. Name the three sections of Sonata form (Sonata Allegro form).

_____   _____   _____

# LESSON 15
# THE ROMANTIC PERIOD
# DVORÁK AND GRIEG

The **ROMANTIC PERIOD** was from approximately 1830-1900. Music of the Romantic Period is the most popular of the four periods of music history. Some characteristics of this music are:

a. **Music became more emotional:** Much of the music of the Romantic period was written about things, people, places, or feelings. The titles in music of the period reflect the mood of the piece (such as *Curious Story* by Heller, *Blindman's Buff* by Schumann, or *Valse Melancolique* by Rebikoff).

b. **Harmonies more complicated:** Composers began to add more colorful notes to their chords, using more chromaticism, and straying from the tonal scale.

c. **Lyric melodies:** Many of the melodies in music of the Romantic period are lovely, singing melodies that have become favorites among music lovers.

d. **Rhythms more complicated:** Music of the Romantic period contains many syncopated rhythms, complicated sixteenth note patterns, dotted rhythms, triplets, cross rhythms (two against three), etc.

This example, from *Reaper's Song* by Schumann, shows these characteristics: A descriptive title, more complex chords, more complicated rhythms, lyric melody.

# EDVARD GRIEG

**Edvard Grieg** was born in Norway in 1843. Although he studied in Leipzig, Germany, he wrote a good deal of music which has a Norwegian flavor, inspired by folk tunes of his country. His *Piano Concerto* and *Peer Gynt Suite* are his most famous works. He also wrote other music for orchestra and solo instruments, including *Lyric Pieces* for piano solo.

He traveled much, working both as a composer and a conductor, until his death in 1907.

# ANTONIN DVORÁK

**Antonin Dvorák** (Da-vor-zhak) was born in 1841, in Prague, Czechoslovakia. He rose from poverty to become one of the most highly regarded composers of the Romantic Period. He began his music studies as a violin student in his home village, but his father wanted him to become a butcher. Dvorák was sent to another town to be an apprentice to his uncle, but his desire for music drew him away from his apprenticeship. In 1857 he began attending the Organ School in Prague, and when he graduated in 1850, began working the first of a wide variety of jobs.

His jobs included playing viola in a dance band and a theatre orchestra, teaching privately, organist of St. Adalberts, and support from the Austrian State Stipendium (due to the strength of several of his compositions). In 1892, Dvorák became director of the National Conservatory of Music in New York, and it was during this time that he composed his famous Ninth Symphony (the *New World Symphony*). He also worked as a professor of composition at the Prague Conservatory.

Dvorák wrote a great deal of orchestral music, including many symphonies, and is also known for his chamber music. His works also include operas, cantatas, oratorios, and other choral works, songs, and concertos. His melodies and rhythms show strong influences of his country's folk music. His life ended in 1904, when he died of a stroke.

Four other Romantic composers are:

**Robert Schumann,** born in Germany, 1810-1856

**Frederick Chopin,** born in Poland, 1810-1849

**Franz Schubert,** born in Austria, 1797-1828

**Johannes Brahms,** born in Germany, 1833-1897

1. List four characteristics of music from the Romantic Period and describe each.

a. _____

_____

_____

b. _____

_____

_____

c. _____

_____

_____

d. _____

_____

_____

2. Complete the following information about each of these composers.

**Edvard Grieg**

Dates of birth and death: _____

Historical Period: _____

Country of birth: _____

Country where some of life was spent: _____

Most famous compositions: _____

Factor that influenced his music: _____

_____

Other works: _____

_____


**Antonin Dvorák**

Dates of birth and death: _____

Historical Period: _____

Country of birth: _____

Positions held: _____

_____

Types of compositions: _____

Things that influenced his musical style: _____

_____

3. Name four other Romantic composers, their places of birth, and their dates of birth and death.

_____    _____    _____

_____    _____    _____

_____    _____    _____

_____    _____    _____

# LESSON 16
# THE 20th and 21st CENTURIES (CONTEMPORARY)
# DELLO-JOIO AND PROKOFIEV

Many changes have taken place in the way music sounds during the 20th and 21st Centuries. The 20th and 21st Centuries are sometimes divided into two style periods: 1900-1950, and 1950-present. Some characteristics of this period are:

a. **Major and minor tonalities avoided**, with non-tonal (not in Major or minor keys) harmonies being used.

b. **Quartal Harmony:** Chords based on the interval of a fourth:

**QUARTAL HARMONY**

c. **Bitonality:** The use of two different keys at the same time:

**BITONALITY**

d. **Polytonality:** The use of many different keys at the same time:

**POLYTONALITY**

e. **Atonality:** No specific key or tonality:

## ATONALITY

f. **Irregular and changing meters:** Composers often use time signatures such as $\frac{5}{4}$ or $\frac{7}{4}$, or change the time signature during the course of the music (complex meter).

g. **Polyphonic texture:** This texture is often used, with the harmonies becoming the result of the interweaving of the melodic lines.

h. **Use of Classical forms:** Composers often write Sonatas, Sonatinas, or other forms which were common during the Classical Period.

This example shows these characteristics: polyphonic texture, changing (complex) meter, avoidance of Major and minor tonalities.

# NORMAN DELLO-JOIO

Born in 1913, **Norman Dello-Joio** was a 20th Century composer from New York City. He studied music at the Julliard School, and for a few years, taught at Sarah Lawrence College in Bronxville, New York.

Some of his well known composition include *Concerto for Harp and Orchestra*, *Ricercari* for piano and orchestra, and *New York Profiles* for orchestra. He won the Pulitzer Prize in Music in 1957 for *Meditations on Ecclesiastes*.

Norman Dello-Joio lived until 2008.

# SERGEI PROKOFIEV

**Sergei Prokofiev** was a 20th Century Russian composer, and lived from 1891 to 1953. He studied music at the St. Petersburg Conservatory in Russia, and toured many countries as a pianist.

Prokofiev's music contains dissonant harmonies and driving rhythmic patterns, which are characteristics of 20th Century music. With these harmonies and rhythms, however, he used traditional forms and tried to write in the style of the Classical Period of music history. This is known as **neo-classic** writing, and several 20th Century composers used this style.

Although he lived in Russia during a time of great political upheaval, Prokofiev's music is often humorous. He wrote several piano concertos, orchestral works, solo piano works, songs, ballets, and many other types of works. He also wrote a set of works for young pianists called *Music for Children*. Children also enjoy listening to one of his most famous works, *Peter and the Wolf*, for orchestra and narrator.

Four other 20th Century composers include:

**Bela Bartók,** born in Hungary, 1881-1945

**Dmitri Shostakovich,** born in Russia, 1906-1975

**Dmitri Kabalevsky,** born in Russia, 1904-1987

**Aaron Copland,** born in U.S.A., 1900-1990

1. List eight characteristics of music from the 20th and 21st Centuries and describe each.

a. _____

_____

_____

b. _____

_____

_____

c. _____

_____

_____

d. _____

_____

_____

e. _____

_____

_____

f. _____

_____

_____

g. _____

_____

_____

h. _____

_____

_____

2. Complete the following information about each of these composers.

**Norman Dello-Joio**

Dates of birth and death: _____

Historical Period: _____

Country of birth: _____

Education: _____

Position held: _____

_____

Award received: _____

_____

Compositions: _____

_____

_____

120

**Sergei Prokofiev**

Dates of birth and death: _____

Historical Period: _____

Country of birth: _____

Education: _____

Style of writing: _____

_____

Types of compositions: _____

_____

Titles of works specifically for children: _____

_____

_____

3. Name four other 20th and 21st Century composers, their places of birth, and their dates of birth and death.

_____    _____    _____

_____    _____    _____

_____    _____    _____

_____    _____    _____

# REVIEW
# LESSONS 8-16

1. Write counts for these phrases, and place accents on the strong beats.

a. From *Venetian Boat Song, Op. 30, No. 6,* by Mendelssohn.

b. From *Sonata, Op. 49, No. 2*, by Beethoven.

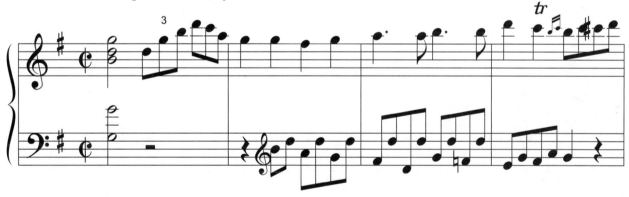

c. From *May, Sweet May,* by Schumann.

2. Define these terms.

a. *allargando* _____

b. *meno mosso* _____

c. *piu mosso* _____

d. *con fuoco* _____

e. *rallentando* _____

f. *ritenuto* _____

g. *senza* _____

h. *sempre* _____

i. *piu* _____

j. *meno* _____

k. *lento* _____

l. *giocoso* _____

m. *grazioso* _____

n. *pesante* _____

o. Alberti bass _____

p. enharmonic _____

q. *...etto* _____

r. *...ino* _____

s. _____

t. _____

u. syncopation _____

v. canon _____

w. Parallel Major and minor _____

x. Relative Major and minor _____

y. sequence _____

z. imitation _____

3. Circle the compositional technique used in each of these examples (repetition, sequence, imitation, or canon), and write the name of the technique on the line above the music.

a. From *Sonata, Op. 49, No. 2,* by Beethoven. _____

b. From *Invention No. 3* by J.S. Bach. _____

c. From *Row Row Row* Your Boat. _____

d. From *Sonata, Op. 49, No. 2,* by Beethoven. _____

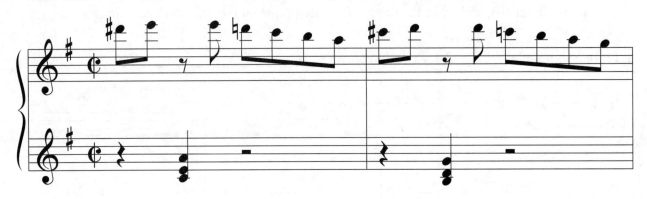

4. Name the four periods of music history and give their approximate dates.

_____  _____

_____  _____

_____  _____

_____  _____

5. Mark each of these statements with T for true or F for false.

_____ Frescobaldi was a Baroque composer.

_____ Dvorák was Czechoslovakian.

_____ Della-Joio is an American Baroque composer.

_____ Grieg wrote *Peer Gynt Suite.*

_____ Haydn wrote many symphonies.

_____ Beethoven could not compose music after he went deaf.

_____ Soler was a Romantic composer.

_____ Prokofiev wrote in neo-Baroque style.

_____ 20th and 21st Century music often uses tonalities other than Major and minor.

_____ Alberti bass is common in music of the Baroque Period.

_____ Haydn and Beethoven are composers of the Classical Period.

6. Define **Meter.** _____

7. Transpose this excerpt from a minuet by Mozart to the key of G Major. Write the transposition on the staff below the music.

8. What term is used for a key change within a composition? _____

9. Name the three sections of Sonata form (Sonata Allegro form).

_____    _____    _____

*This page has purposely been left blank*

Score: _____  **REVIEW TEST**  Perfect Score: 100
Passing Score: 70

1. Name each Major and minor key signature, and notate the tonic triad for each key. (The first one is given.) (7 points)

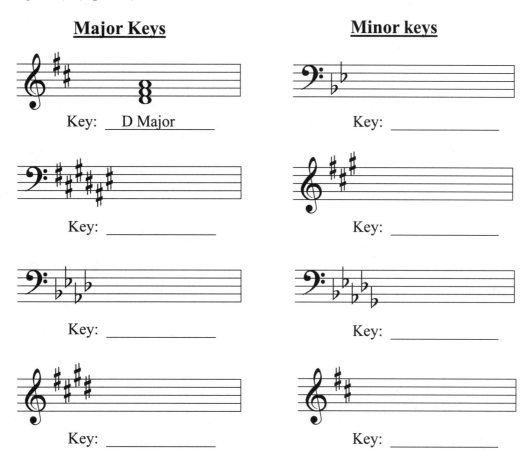

**Major Keys**

Key:    D Major

Key: _____

Key: _____

Key: _____

**Minor keys**

Key: _____

Key: _____

Key: _____

Key: _____

2. Add sharps or flats to complete each of these minor scales. (Do not use a key signature. Place the accidentals before the notes.) (3 points)

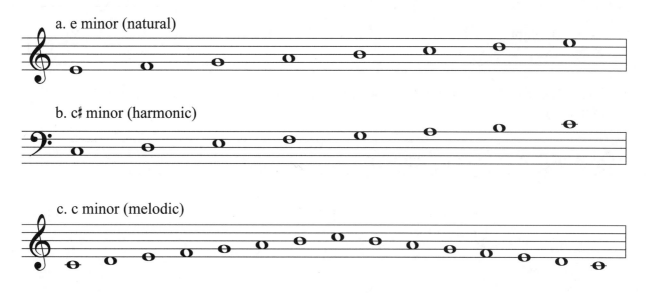

a. e minor (natural)

b. c# minor (harmonic)

c. c minor (melodic)

128

3. Name these intervals. (The first one is given.) (9 points)

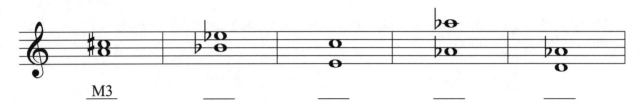

M3 ___ ___ ___ ___

___ ___ ___ ___ ___

4. Complete these triads. (The first one is given.) (4 points)

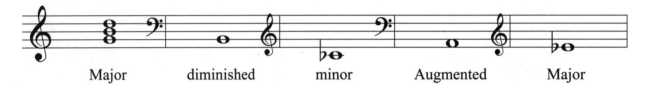

Major    diminished    minor    Augmented    Major

5. Write this chord progression. (The tonic triad is given.) (4 points)

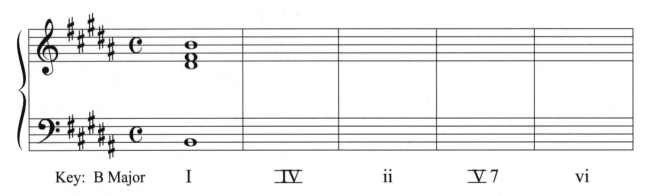

Key: B Major    I    IV    ii    V 7    vi

6. Write Dominant Seventh chords in each of the following keys. (The first one is given.) (5 points)

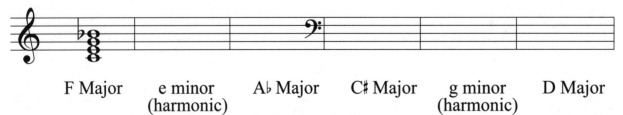

F Major    e minor    A♭ Major    C♯ Major    g minor    D Major
(harmonic)                      (harmonic)

7. Write the time signature for each of the following rhythmic patterns. (The first one is given.) (4 points)

a.

b.

c.

d.

e.

8. Match the following terms with the correct definitions. (Put the number of the term next to the definition.) (8 points)

1. *giocoso*         _____ heavily

2. canon          _____ without

3. *meno mosso*     _____ joyfully

4. *pesante*         _____ always

5. *ritenuto*        _____ less motion

6. *senza*          _____ immediately slower

7. *sempre*         _____ slowly

8. *lento*          _____ strict imitation of an entire theme

9. The following example is from *French Suite No. 6: Polonaise,* by J.S. Bach. Answer the questions about the music. (14 points)

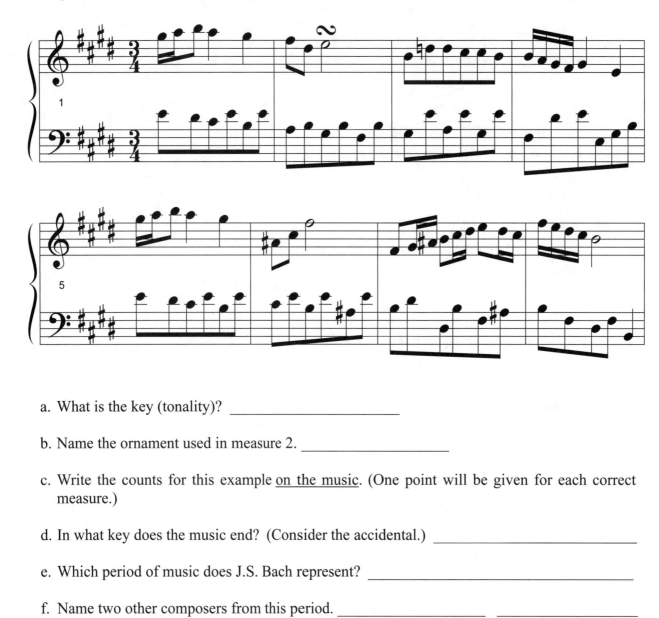

a. What is the key (tonality)? _____

b. Name the ornament used in measure 2. _____

c. Write the counts for this example <u>on the music</u>. (One point will be given for each correct measure.)

d. In what key does the music end? (Consider the accidental.) _____

e. Which period of music does J.S. Bach represent? _____

f. Name two other composers from this period. _____  _____

10. The following example is from *Sonatina, Op. 20, No. 1*, by Kuhlau. Answer the questions about the music. (9 points)

a.  What is the key (tonality)? _____

b.  Name each circled chord with its root, quality, Roman numeral, and figured bass.

|  | **Root and Quality** | **Roman Numeral and Figured Bass** |
|---|---|---|
| Triad a. | _____ | _____ |
| Triad b. | _____ | _____ |
| Triad c. | _____ | _____ |
| Triad d. | _____ | _____ |
| Triad e. | _____ | _____ |

c. Name the cadence in measure 4. _____

d. Name the cadence in measures 7-8. _____

e. Which period of history does Kuhlau represent? _____

11. The following example is from *Mazurka, Op. 68, No. 3 (Posth.)* by Chopin. Answer the questions about the music. (10 points)

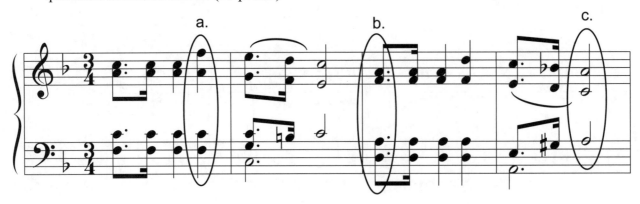

a. What is the key (tonality)? _____

b. Name each circled chord with its root, quality, Roman numeral, and figured bass.

|  | **Root and Quality** | **Roman Numeral and Figured Bass** |
|---|---|---|
| Triad a. | _____ | _____ |
| Triad b. | _____ | _____ |
| Triad c. | _____ | _____ |
| Triad d. | _____ | _____ |
| Triad e. | _____ | _____ |

c. Name the cadence at the end of the example. _____

d. Which period of music history does Chopin represent? _____

e. Name two other composers from the same period. _____  _____

12. Answer the questions below about this musical example. (10 points)

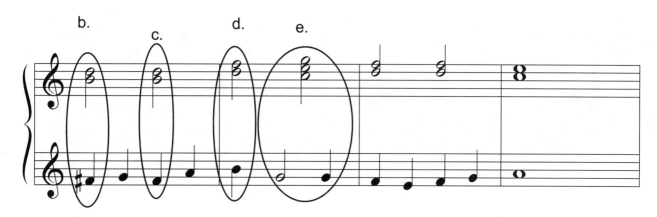

a. According to the key signature and the last chord, what is the key (tonality)? _____

b. Name each circled chord with its root, quality, and figured bass.

   Triad a. _____

   Triad b. _____

   Triad c. _____

   Triad d. _____

   Triad e. _____

c. What type of scale movement is used in the left hand in measures 1-4? _____

d. This example avoids major and minor tonality. Which historical period is known for this

   characteristic? _____

e. Name two composers from this period. _____  _____

13. The following example is from Sonatina, Hob. XVI:10: Trio, by Haydn. Answer the questions about the music. (13 points)

a. What is the key (tonality)? _____

b. Circle the correct way to play the trill in measure 4.

c. Name each circled interval with its quality and number.

  1. _____   2. _____   3. _____   4. _____   5. _____   6. _____   7. _____   8. _____

d. Name the period of music history which Haydn represents. _____

e. Name two other composers from this same period. _____   _____

# MODE CHART

| Name of Mode | Scale Degree | Interval |
|---|---|---|
| Ionian | First | P1 |
| Dorian | Second | M2 |
| Phrygian | Third | M3 |
| Lydian | Fourth | P4 |
| Mixolydian | Fifth | P5 |
| Aeolian | Sixth | M6 |
| Locrian | Seventh | M7 |

To determine which sharps or flats are in a mode:

Go down the interval for that mode, and use the sharps or flats from the resulting key signature.

For example: To determine the key signature for Dorian Mode on F:

a. Go down a M2 from F  (Answer: E♭)
b. Use the key signature from E♭ Major, but begin and end on F
   (Answer: F  G  A♭  B♭  C  D  E♭  F)

To determine the name of a given mode:

Find the Major key signature by looking at the sharps or flats included in the mode.

Count up from the name of the key signature to the starting note of the mode.

Match the name of the mode with the scale degree on which the mode begins.

For example:  To determine the name of this mode:  E  F♯  G♯  A  B  C♯  D  E

a. The sharps are F♯, G♯, and C♯. Put in key signature order:  F♯, C♯, G♯. Key of A Major
b. Beginning on A, count up to the starting note of the mode:  A to E is five notes, or the fifth.
c. The mode which begins on the fifth scale degree is Mixolydian.

# REFERENCES

Apel, Willi. *Harvard Dictionary of Music, Second Edition.* Cambridge, Massachussetts: Belknap Press of Harvard University Press, 1972.

Arnold, Denis, ed. *The New Oxford Companion to Music, Volumes 1 and 2.* New York: Oxford University Press, 1983.

Music Teachers' Association of California. *Certificate of Merit Piano Syllabus.* San Francisco: Music Teachers' Association of California, 1992.

Music Teachers' Association of California. *Certificate of Merit Piano Syllabus.* Ontario, Canada: Frederick Harris Music Co., Limited, 1997.

Music Teachers' Association of California. *Certificate of Merit Piano Syllabus.* San Francisco: Music Teachers' Association of California, 2007.

Russell, John. *A History of Music for Young People.* Toronto, Canada: Clark, Irwin & Company Limited, 1965.

Sadie, Stanley, ed. *The New Grove Dictionary of Music and Musicians.* Washington, D.C.: Grove's Dictionaries of Music Inc., 1980.

# Basics of Keyboard Theory and Guide to AP Theory
# ORDER FORM

NAME_____

ADDRESS_____

CITY_____STATE_____ZIP_____

PHONE_____E-MAIL_____

| QTY | ITEM | COST | TOTAL |
|-----|------|------|-------|
| | **Preparatory Level** | **9.50** | |
| | **Level 1** | **9.50** | |
| | **Level 2** | **9.50** | |
| | **Level 3** | **9.95** | |
| | **Level 4** | **9.95** | |
| | **Level 5** | **10.50** | |
| | **Level 6** | **10.50** | |
| | **Level 7** | **10.95** | |
| | **Level 8** | **11.95** | |
| | **Level 9** | **12.95** | |
| | **Level 10** | **12.50** | |
| | **Answer Book, Levels P-10** | **11.95** | |
| | **Julie Johnson's Guide to AP Music Theory** | **39.95** | |

| | |
|---|---|
| **Sub-Total** | |
| Calif. Residents: Sales Tax | |
| **Shipping** | |
| **TOTAL** | |

Shipping Rates:
  1-5 Items.........$5.00
  6-10 Items.......$6.00
  11 or more.......$7.00

Order online, or mail form with payment.  Make checks payable to:
**J. Johnson Music Publications**
5062 Siesta Lane
Yorba Linda, CA 92886
714-961-0257   Fax:  714-242-9350
www.bktmusic.com   info@bktmusic.com
Prices subject to change.  Check www.bktmusic.com for current information.